Spirituality and Stuff

The Reflections of an Addictions Chaplain

By

Gregory P. Gabriel

Foreword by Robert H. Albers, Ph.D.

ISBN: 0-7596-2807-6

This book is printed on acid free paper.

1stBooks - rev. 10/29/01

The excerpt from the pamphlet *Three Talks to Medical Societies by Bill W., co-founder of A.A.*, and brief excerpts from the following texts: *Alcoholics Anonymous, As Bill Sees It, Dr. Bob and the Good Oldtimers, Twelve Steps and Twelve Traditions, Alcoholics Anonymous Comes of Age, Came to Believe, and 'Pass It On'* are reprinted with permission of Alcoholics Anonymous World Services, Inc. (A.A.W.S.). Permission to use this material does not mean that A.A.W.S. has reviewed or approved the contents of this publication, or that A.A.W.S. necessarily agrees with the views expressed herein. A.A. is a program of recovery from alcoholism only. Use of this material in connection with programs and activities which are patterned after A.A., but which address other problems or concerns, or in any other non-A.A. context, does not imply otherwise.

iv

Dedicated to my wife, Joanne,
and to our sons, Tim and Chris

Table of Contents

Foreword by Robert H. Albers, Ph.D. xi
Preface xv
Acknowledgements.. xvii
Preliminary Notes xix

A Lesson in Humility.. 1
About Violence... 4
Alcohol and the Norwegian Immigrants.............................. 6
Alcoholism and Financial Problems 9
An Angry Lutheran Minister 12
An Unsettling Thought.. 15
Anonymity 17
Be Sly 20
Bill W.? A Ladies' Man? 22
Boredom 25
Can a Person be a Higher Power?....................................... 28
Coffee 30
Coincidences... 32
Compulsive Gambling and Sex 35
Coping With Christmas 37
Courtesy.. 40
Divine Dissatisfaction... 43
Fancy Words and Lugubrious People.................................. 45
Fear of Falling 48
Getting Too Close to the Drink 50
Go Ahead and Call the Bishop 52
Guidance and Checking... 55
Handwriting on the Wall 57
How Do You Get the Spiritual Part of the Program? 59
How to Hear a Fifth Step 62
Hypocrisy and the Church 65
In the Days Before A.A. 68

Not a Very Spiritual Person 70
On Our Knees 72
Organized Religion 75
Piles 77
Religion Revisited 80
Remembering William James 82
Revelation 85
Rigorous Reading 88
Silence 91
Some Provocative Thoughts About Prayer and Meditation 94
Spiritual Awakenings and the Animal Kingdom 97
Spirituality Versus Religion 99
Suicide 102
Taking a Tunk 104
Tales from Papua New Guinea 106
Tears 108
That Dawg Don't Hunt 110
The Anatomy of a Grief Letter 113
The Angel and the Tour Guide 116
The Church is My Mother 119
The Empty Pew 122
The Greater Challenge 125
The Incarnation 128
The Legitimate Use of the Word "Spiritual" 130
The Man Who Would Not Hurry 132
The Meeting in the Basement 134
The Spirit or the Spirits? 137
The Tractor Man 139
Tight Pants 142
Twin Tornadoes 145
What is a Spiritual Awakening? 147
What the Church Might Learn from A.A. 149
Workaholism 151
You Do Not Have to Answer the Telephone Every
    Time It Rings 153

Endnotes 155
Appendix A: 12 Steps of Alcoholics Anonymous................... 163
Appendix B: 12 Traditions of Alcoholics Anonymous 165
Appendix C: 12 Steps of Gamblers Anonymous.................... 167
Bibliography 169
About the Author... 173

x

Foreword

A potpourri of poignant insights, seasoned wisdom, and inspirational reflections characterize this compendium of meditative writings by Chaplain Greg Gabriel. The volume is published under the general title of *Spirituality and Stuff: The Reflections of an Addictions Chaplain*. The thrust of the work as a whole is an effort to integrate the spirituality of the 12-Step program of recovery with the ecstasies and exigencies of everyday life. Chaplain Gabriel, furthermore, draws deeply from the well of his own theological tradition. His role as a chaplain in a treatment center, coupled with his role as a pastor in rural America, makes for a rich combination of experiences from which to garner the nuggets of wisdom contained in this volume.

As I read through the various meditations that feature the core of 12-Step spirituality as appropriated in the experience and life of an addictions chaplain, the thoughts were reminiscent of those articulated in the *Twenty-Four Hours a Day* meditation book. Chaplain Gabriel's publication features succinct and pithy commentaries on addiction, recovery, and spirituality. What sets this volume apart from others is the perspective from which it is written, namely, that of a chaplain serving in such a setting, as opposed to a person in recovery. The angle of vision in this publication is unique, as the author functions as a chaplain and a pastor issuing commentary on what he experiences and observes from his perspective.

Chaplain Gabriel extrapolates wisdom from a variety of sources. It is obvious that he is well acquainted with the basic literature in recovery, as evidenced in the footnotes he cites. Over the years of his service in this dual capacity as chaplain and pastor, he has a plethora of stories and anecdotes from which to draw that brings a powerful note of reality to what he writes. His writing models the principal virtues of the recovery program, as honesty, transparency, candor, and vulnerability characterize many of the meditations that appear in this volume. It would be possible to assemble these meditations around each of the 12 Steps of recovery, and one would have in hand not only an inspirational compilation of meditations, but also a significant profile of the author's own character and spirituality.

The reflections are terse, and each can be read in a matter of a few minutes. The author goes to the heart of the matter, devoid of unnecessary verbiage. Like the recovery program, Chaplain Gabriel's thoughts are profound, but kept simple in relating the heart of each message to a story, an observation, or an experience that the reader can easily identify with in her or his own life. As a professional, he is at one level an objective outsider, but as a practitioner who has not only thought about, but lived out the principles of the program in his own life, he is very much an insider. This rare combination of an objective observer, as well as an insightful insider, lends credibility and congruency to his writing.

These reflections are appropriate for a wide range of people, not only clergy or chaplains. The truths and insights expressed are applicable to the human situation, irrespective of a person's station in life. While the focal point of concentration is recovery from addiction, any reader could read these reflections and identify with the content if she or he is honest about the reality of the human condition.

This volume is probably best read very slowly. It is not to be read in one sitting; rather, each meditation or reflection lends itself as a stimulus to further reflection and elaboration on the part of the reader. I found myself identifying with many of the things that were written, and would pause to allow my own memory and imagination to become active. A thought, a feeling, or an idea is presented in such a way that the reader is encouraged to engage in further meditation about the truth that has been written for one's own life. It was good to savor the flavor of what was written and to allow oneself the privilege of brooding about the insight or truth. Thus, for me, Chaplain

Gabriel's writing became a catalyst for my own meditative reflection, which is what distinguishes him as a gifted writer.

As a former professor of pastoral care in a theological seminary, it is always gratifying to see one's students flower and flourish in ministry. As a theological student, Greg was always thoughtful, reflective, and insightful. I recall his presence in my class on chemical dependency, and his eagerness to involve himself in a clinical setting where he continued to grow and to learn as a chaplain and pastor. These meditations are indicative of the depth he has reached in understanding both the recovery program as well as the Christian tradition as a pastoral theologian and pastoral caregiver. It is my hope and prayer that he will continue to share his reflections in the future with others. His poignant stories and examples, coupled with his own experiences and expressions of spirituality and recovery, will continue to increase with the passage of time. May the Spirit that inspired him to write about those captivated by the "spirits" continue to inspire him, and those with whom he works, to greater health and wholeness.

Robert H. Albers, Ph.D.
Minneapolis, Minnesota

Preface

I have written a series of articles that are gathered loosely around the theme of "Spirituality and Stuff." These articles are intended to say something about the subject of spirituality and recovery from addictions (with a dash of irreverence to make it interesting). Perhaps the title *Spirituality and Stuff* calls for exposition.

Please understand that I am using the word *stuff* advisedly. I am not tossing the word around recklessly, like an adolescent who remarks, "We went to the mall and *stuff*."

On the contrary, I intend this word in a more profound and mature sense, like when a genetic researcher makes the claim that "DNA is the very *stuff* of life." I am employing the word *stuff* not as a useless generalization, but as a word that points to something essential, yet beyond description: Spirituality and *Stuff*.

As for that other term—spirituality—I shall confess from the outset that I cannot say exactly what it means. You might assume that a chaplain at an addictions treatment center (like myself) would be something of an authority on the subject of spirituality, but I am not. For some reason, I cannot seem to come up with a satisfying definition for the word.

Come to think of it, I believe that I became a pastor (and a chaplain) in the first place, not because my comprehension of spirituality was so complete, but because I felt compelled by some questions about spirituality. Perhaps the articles which follow represent some of my own quest to come to terms with the meaning of spirituality.

I once had a college English professor who asserted, "A good writer is one for whom writing is difficult." His point, I believe, is that good writing is not something that comes quickly or easily, but rather something that involves toil and struggle. By analogy, I suppose you could say that I became a pastor primarily because I did not understand the concept of spirituality, and felt the need to labor over it. I like to think that some of the writing I have done about spirituality has helped me to clarify my own thinking on the subject.

It seems to me that the 12-Step programs have always placed great store in *spirituality*—even though the word is rarely defined with precision, or by any consensus of opinion. I do not think that there is an all-sufficient definition for the term. Alcoholics Anonymous tends to *hint* at what spirituality might be about: for example, when one really takes notice of a robin in the spring, for the first time. A.A. prefers to encourage people to find their own understanding of spirituality, which, I suppose, is why the word spirituality remains rather vague and imprecise...not unlike the word "stuff."

Perhaps I am being a bit coy when I claim that I do not know what the word spirituality really means. Frankly, I do not think that anyone can come up with an all-encompassing definition of the word spirituality, but anyone can talk about "what-spirituality-means-to-me." I myself like to think of spirituality as "the capacity to give and receive love." Spirituality, I believe, is vitally concerned with how we relate to one another.

Some might object that this personal definition fails to take into account God or a Higher Power, but I figure that God is *implied* in any human relationship. In other words, it is the presence of God that makes community possible; on the other hand, the absence of human intimacy is akin to the absence of God. In short, God is the "stuff" of which relationships are made. There you have it: an introduction to the subject of Spirituality and Stuff.

An A.A. publication puts it like this: "I cannot say that I have found God as I understand Him, but rather that I have faith in Something which remains a mystery to me and which I continue to seek."[1]

Acknowledgements

As I prepare to send this book to be printed, I am aware that its contents reflect the conversations I have had through the years with a wide variety of people, to whom I am indebted. I have learned about spirituality and recovery from addictions, primarily, from the many patients I have encountered during my years of work as a chaplain at Project Turnabout (an addictions treatment center in Granite Falls, Minnesota) and at Hazelden (a chemical dependency treatment center near Center City, Minnesota). The insights I have gained from fellow staff members at these treatment centers are also represented in these pages. I am grateful to the good people of A.A. and Al-Anon for the things they have taught me about the process of recovery from addictions—including those people I have met through literature.

I appreciate the sabbatical that was granted to me by my parish—Mandt and Jevnaker Lutheran Churches of rural Montevideo, Minnesota—so that I could complete this book. I am grateful to Pastor John Beem, who graciously covered my parish duties during my writing sabbatical, and to Gwen Degner, who combed through the manuscript with the eyes of a grammarian. Finally, I am thankful to my wife, Joanne, for helping to prepare this manuscript for publication, and for her overall support of this writing project.

Gregory P. Gabriel

Preliminary Notes

William G. Wilson, who was a businessman from New York, and Dr. Robert H. Smith, a physician from Akron, Ohio, founded the Alcoholics Anonymous movement in 1935. Commonly, they are known as Bill W. and Dr. Bob.

Bill W. was the primary author of the basic handbook of the Alcoholics Anonymous program. Although its formal title is *Alcoholics Anonymous*, it is known affectionately as the "Big Book."

Both Bill W. and Dr. Bob had backgrounds in the Oxford Group before they began to piece together the Alcoholics Anonymous program. The Oxford Group was a form of small-group Christianity which flourished in the United States and Europe in the1920's and 1930's. The Oxford Group endeavored to revive the principles of early Christianity. The founders of the Alcoholics Anonymous program eventually pulled away from the Oxford Group, and established their own fellowship, specifically for the support of alcoholics.

The Alcoholics Anonymous program (A.A.) has spawned a wide variety of other 12-Step programs—including Al-Anon, which is a support group for the family members of alcoholics; Narcotics Anonymous (N.A.); Gamblers Anonymous (G.A.); and Gam-Anon, which is a support group for the families of compulsive gamblers.

A Lesson in Humility

I recall my first golf lesson. I have played some mini-golf in my time, but I had never swung a golf club in earnest until I made my debut on the golf course. I figured that there must be something *spiritual* about this sport (many people see it as an alternative to going to church on Sunday mornings, you know) so I decided to find out about this game for myself.

As I parked near the country club and removed my borrowed bag of clubs from the trunk, I noticed an assembly of women standing near the beginning of the course. It must be Ladies' Day or something, I surmised. I wondered where my class would meet. When I inquired in the clubhouse, however, I learned that the semi-circle of women at the start of the course was indeed the group I was seeking.

Oh.

I sidled up to the flock with chagrin in my heart and the bag of clubs dangling from my shoulder. I counted the women who were present for the class: 30. Then I counted the men who were interspersed: three, including myself. I was outnumbered exactly 10-1. Most of the women seemed to be on the other side of "middle age," too, unless I merely imagined as much. (For a minute, I thought I was at an Al-Anon meeting.)

About that time, a svelte young man with a clipboard stepped to the fore, and introduced himself as the instructor. He launched into a brisk orientation to this genteel pastime, beginning with how to hold a club properly: the "baseball grip" versus the "split grip" as opposed to the "wrap."

Having explained how to clasp a golf club properly, the instructor said to us, "Now I would like you to take out your nine-iron, or your wedge, and come with me."

For an instant, I froze.

My mind was racing. I thought, "Now when I am asked to take out my nine-iron or my wedge—does this mean that I am to

1

take out my nine-iron *or else* my wedge—or does this mean that the club called a nine-iron can also be referred to as a wedge?"

I have been called a "well-defended" individual. We well-defended people do not like to do things that might appear foolish, but then we do not care to ask potentially foolish questions which might betray our ignorance, either. What to do? What to do? One club or two?

Someone once told me about a principle called W.T.B.D.— an acronym which stands for "Willingness To Be a Dummy." I am not in my element when I am on a golf course; therefore, almost anything I do or say involves a risk, the peril of making a mistake, the danger that someone might think I am stupid. According to the W.T.B.D. principle, however, it is okay to err. It is acceptable to ask dumb questions.

What did I do? Well, what would you do in such a crucial situation? I cast a furtive glance toward the grandmotherly type on my right. She fiddled with her clubs for a moment, and then with a flourish of authority unsheathed a single weapon, and set off after the instructor at a crisp gait. I did the same.

We did a little "chipping" near the practice holes with our nine-irons (Is that the same as a wedge?) but then came the real test. The instructor produced a seven-iron and prepared to demonstrate how to use it. He stepped up to the ball, and gracefully drove it high into the sky and far down the fairway. The class "oohed" admiringly.

Then it was our turn to try. I dug in. I used the split grip. For all I know the entire class was studying my form, but I was intent upon that ball. With a spirited whack (and on my first attempt!) I spanked the ball farther and truer than even the instructor had managed. The ball soared with majesty, and plopped down near the green 175 years away...NNNOT! Actually, I took a murderous chop at the ball and succeeded in carving out a chunk of earth the size of a cereal bowl. I barely grazed the ball itself.

The instructor, who was looking on, remarked, "Yeah, it's a humbling game." I remembered hearing once that the word "humble" literally means "near to the ground." I got near to the ground all right!

Secretly, I had been wondering if I might have some kind of latent gift for this game, a hidden talent waiting to spring forth once I applied the club to the ball. Like a beautiful statue yearning to be set free from a slab of marble, I was thinking that I might be really good at golf if I gave it a chance—but I was disabused of this notion with the terrible suddenness of a deep divot.

I have found that whether you are seeking to learn the game of golf, or whether you are seeking to learn whatever it takes to stay sober in A.A., some essential spiritual tasks are these: 1) surrendering terminal uniqueness (the conviction that I am different); 2) becoming humble (or teachable); and 3) becoming a regular guy (not an expert).

This business about becoming truly *spiritual* is really about becoming truly *human*—on the golf course or anywhere else.

By the way, I am available for foursomes.

About Violence

For most of the afternoon, he had been sitting alone in the basement, watching television and drinking beer. Several times, his wife had come down to berate him, but he ignored her umbrage and kept on drinking. This time, however, she yanked his hair from behind, in a desperate bid to win his attention. In one swift maneuver, he whirled and broke her grip, then sprang to his feet, and punched her full-force in the eye.

The woman fell down on her back, clutching her face. From the moment of impact, the tissue around her eye began to swell and to darken with blood. The man felt a tremendous surge of guilt the very instant his fist met her face. He said that he was sorry, and helped her to sit on the couch. Then the man scrambled upstairs to the refrigerator to get some ice for her, wrapped it in a washcloth, and handed it to her plaintively. Again he apologized.

Then he left the house.

This same ugly scene is played out again and again, with infinite variations. The characters might be different, and the setting may change—but the abuse of alcohol is the same, and the violent consequences are familiar. Physical abuse is a burgeoning reality in our society; frequently, it correlates with the misuse of alcohol. Many people, when intoxicated, will commit acts of savagery that would be inconceivable if they were sober.

Some years ago, I applied for a job which required that I be fingerprinted. I was referred to the county jail for this particular service. The jailer was amused by my request to be fingerprinted, but he also agreed to help me. He pressed my fingers, one at a time, into an inkpad, and then rolled each finger on a card.

"Just relax," he advised me. "You're too tight." "Let your hand go limp," he directed. He repeated these instructions to me several times. A trace of annoyance even crept into his voice. "You're too tense," he chided.

After he had completed the task, he pointed me to a sink and stack of paper towels. His irritation was gone now. "I guess it has been a long time since I inked somebody who wasn't tanked up," he remarked. I took this to mean that most of the people who find their way into his professional company are drunk, and therefore more pliable at the inkpad. Alcohol does have a way of loosening a person's joints, as well as a person's baser impulses, like the proclivity to punch.

Researchers claim that we live in the most violent developed country in the world. Certainly, the abuse of alcohol can be conducive to violence—but it is only one of many contributing factors. Violence is a complex problem, with various potential causes, one of them being drunkenness.

An author by the name of Thomas Merton lays an entirely different perspective on the problem of violence, however. Merton once penned these words: "The rush and pressure of modern life are a form, perhaps the most common form, of its innate violence. To allow oneself to be carried away by a multitude of conflicting concerns, to surrender to too many demands, to commit oneself to too many projects, to want to help everyone in everything is to succumb to violence."[2] Merton sees a correlation between the use of extreme force and the frenzied pace of modern life.

According to this line of reasoning, the social problem of violence is traceable not just to the abuse of alcohol, or to the disease of alcoholism, but also to our bustling schedules. Merton observes that we are violently busy people. Perhaps the roots of violence are intertwined with our own primal haste.

If violence often relates to the abuse of alcohol (and I believe it does) then the problem is mostly "out there" somewhere. If violence also relates to our hurried lifestyles (which also seems plausible) then we all have something to ponder.

Alcohol and the Norwegian Immigrants

I spend half of my work week as a chaplain at an addictions treatment center. In the course of my work, I do a lot of talking with alcoholics. I spend the rest of my work week as the pastor of two rural Lutheran congregations. Most of the members of these churches seem to be of Norwegian descent (like myself). One of these congregations observed its centennial not long ago.

In anticipation of this special occasion, I did some reading about the history of Norwegian immigration. In fact, I worked my way through a book called *The Promise of America* by Odd S. Lovoll. As I sifted through some of the history of Norwegian immigration, I came across some interesting information about the establishment of Norwegian Lutheran churches in this country, but I also found out more than I expected to learn about the abuse of alcohol among the Norwegian immigrants. Somehow, my two part-time jobs no longer seemed as different from one another as they once seemed.

According to the aforementioned historian, many of the Norwegian immigrants were experienced drinkers. Liquor was plentiful back in "The Old Country." Indeed, many of the farmers in Norway were in the habit of bringing their alcoholic beverages out into the fields where they worked. The abuse of alcohol was already a ponderous problem in Norway by the mid-1860's, when the first great surge of immigrants made their way to the United States.

The immigrants did not represent a cross-section of Norwegian society; predominantly, they were the peasants and the poor and the common laborers. The historian suggests that a disproportionate number of the immigrants seemed to have trouble with alcohol, too. "Many people who lost both home and farm from addiction to alcohol sought emigration as the only way out," notes Lovoll.[3]

I take this to mean that many of the Norwegians who felt free to pull up stakes and relocate to a new land were those who had lost their livelihoods to their hard drinking back in Norway. In other words, many of the immigrants were making what we in the treatment industry call a "geographical escape."

In time, the Norwegian immigrants gained a reputation in this country as hearty consumers of alcohol. Some of the tales about their drinking and brawling and debauchery have been exaggerated, the historian points out, but the Norwegian immigrants clearly had their troubles with booze. The historian asserts that these immigrants seemed to do their drinking in a more conspicuous fashion than many of their ethnic neighbors in the United States.

Frequently, the Lutheran pastors would scold the Norwegian immigrants about their drinking—they even refused to give Holy Communion to anyone who worked in a tavern—but their efforts to discourage drinking, for the most part, were in vain. The habit of drinking was too deeply ingrained in the heritage of the Norwegian immigrants.

Many Norwegian immigrants loved their beer and whiskey, but there were other Norwegian immigrants who hated alcohol with a passion. By the late 1870's, the temperance movement reached the Norwegian immigrants in the rural areas of the United States. The Norwegian immigrant communities embraced the temperance cause with some of the same verve that they had otherwise reserved for drinking. These immigrants talked and wrote about the problems associated with drinking. They debated the issue, and even pressed for new legislation concerning alcohol. Some of the Norwegian immigrant women were so zealous about the temperance movement that they seized axes and destroyed saloons.

The historian repeats an intriguing claim: "Norwegians had made a greater contribution to the temperance cause than any other nationality within the boundaries of America."[4] When the temperance movement eventuated in Prohibition in 1920, many referred to it as "Norwegian" legislation.

Disclaimer: I am not suggesting that *all* Norwegian immigrants either had drinking problems or passionate

7

objections to alcohol. Rather, I am saying that the Norwegian immigrants, on the whole, brought more than Lutheran churches to the United States. They also brought some of their own deep issues with alcohol.

Alcoholism and Financial Problems

"The men who cry for money and shelter before
conquering alcohol, are on the wrong track."[5]

Most people who come to treatment for chemical
dependency seem to have money problems. A few who enter
treatment are on solid financial footing, but they seem to
represent the exception to the rule. Generally speaking, people
who have some robust source of income still have some "room to
run," and therefore are not ready to make changes in their lives.

I remember a fellow who came to treatment as an alternative
to jail. He would pace the corridors of the treatment facility,
muttering about how he should be "out there" making money so
he could pay his bills. "How am I supposed to focus on my
treatment," he snapped, "when I have car payments to make?"

His question calls to mind a quote from Bill W., who
remarked, "Most alcoholics have said they had no troubles that
money would not cure."[6] Bill W. himself was acquainted with
financial hardship, and yet he came to this conclusion: "For us,
material well-being always follows spiritual progress; it never
precedes."[7]

The A.A. movement itself was born of financial deprivation.
A.A. had its origin in 1935, in the thick of the Great Depression,
when one-fourth of all American workers was unemployed. In
those days, Bill W. was a stock analyst from New York who was
determined to make a "killing" on Wall Street. Because of his
drinking problems, however, he never did strike it rich in the
stock market. Instead, his wife supported them both with her job
as a clerk in a department store. It always rankled Bill W. that he
could not be the breadwinner for his family.

The other co-founder of A.A. was Dr. Bob, a physician from
Akron, Ohio, whose medical practice had been reduced to almost
nothing by his alcoholism. When a business trip took Bill W. to
Akron, where he first met Dr. Bob, the two discovered that they
had more in common than their drinking problems: both had

severe financial problems, as well. These two men had the insight, however, to recognize their financial crises as a symptom of a deeper issue, namely alcoholism.

Bill W. and Dr. Bob struggled to pull together the A.A program without any semblance of financial security in their lives. After he had been working with other alcoholics for five years, Dr. Bob was 60 years old, strapped for money, and facing retirement. The bank was threatening to foreclose on his house in Akron.

Meanwhile, in New York, the bank did turn Bill W. and his wife out of their home. They were not only without jobs and without a car, but now without a house, as well. Bill W. and his wife were forced to move in with one set of friends after another. They moved 51 times in 1939-40.[8] Bill's wife sat down in a stairway in Grand Central Station one day and wept because they had no home of their own.

The founders of A.A. lived "hand-to-mouth" in those early years, and still the A.A. movement sprang forth, in spite of their poverty. Perhaps the A.A. movement even sprang forth *because* of their poverty.

"'All this happened,' Dr. Bob said, 'at a time when everybody was broke, awfully broke. It was probably much easier for us to be successful when broke than it would have been if we'd had a checking account apiece....I think now that it was providentially arranged.'"[9]

The A.A. program grew without the benefit of financial stability. Bill W., who was sorely in need of employment, was offered a job as a counselor to alcoholics at Towns Hospital in New York, but fellow members of A.A. urged him not to take it, lest "professionalism" taint the A.A. program. Bill W. and his confreres also appealed to John D. Rockefeller for financial assistance, but Rockefeller turned them down. Rockefeller explained that he was concerned that money might "spoil" the A.A. movement.

Both Dr. Bob and Bill W. did accomplish financial solvency in their lifetimes, but only after they had achieved sobriety. Dr.

Bob's medical practice picked up during World War II, when many younger doctors were serving overseas; Bill W. made a princely sum from royalties from the Big Book, which he authored. "We should not seek material things first," according to *Twenty-Four Hours a Day,* "but seek spiritual things first and the material things will come to us, as we honestly work for them."[10]

An Angry Lutheran Minister

Frank Buchman was a Lutheran minister. He lived in Philadelphia a century ago. Buchman was a severe young preacher of German descent. He was a hard-nosed sort. He never smoked or drank alcoholic beverages or married.

Buchman supervised an orphanage in Philadelphia until he got into a disagreement with the trustees of that institution, and resigned in rancor. In a huff, he boarded a ship bound for England. While he was in Keswich, England in 1908, however, he happened to hear a sermon from a Salvation Army preacher.[11] The homily moved him so deeply that he felt compelled to write letters of amends to the people with whom he had argued. This initiative served to assuage his profound bitterness.

In the glow of his new freedom from resentment, Buchman wanted very much to share his spiritual awakening with others. He was convinced that people needed to return to the essentials of what he considered "primitive Christianity." Buchman launched a crusade that emphasized Absolute Honesty, Absolute Purity, Absolute Unselfishness, and Absolute Love. He set out to rouse the world.

Rev. Buchman was an idealistic man, but he was also an effective leader. His strategy was to influence society by appealing to those who possessed wealth and power, or at least the people who seemed destined for social prominence. He hoped that the masses would follow their lead. Buchman took his cause to the student body of prestigious Oxford University, where he found a receptive audience. Within a few years, his effort to re-kindle the spirit of the early Christian church had outgrown the university scene, and he had developed a substantial following both in Europe and the United States.

Buchman insisted that people needed to return to a rudimentary form of Christianity, which included: 1) a surrender before God; 2) making an inventory of their sins; 3) confessing their sins to another person; 4) making amends; 5) helping other people without expecting to be paid; and 6) the practice of prayer.

In the early 1920's, the Buchmanites (as his followers sometimes were called) met in small "house parties."[12] People were not expected to leave their own churches in order to participate in Buchman's fellowship. They simply gathered to talk about their personal struggles, and to listen quietly for God's guidance. By the mid-1930's, however, these meetings had become larger and larger, until conventions drew tens of thousands of the faithful.[13]

The people who came to these meetings discussed all sorts of personal and spiritual issues with one another. Some of the Buchmanites talked about their drinking problems. Those who struggled specifically with alcohol gradually formed their own support groups within the structure of the Buchmanites' movement. Eventually, they withdrew entirely from the Buchmanites.

The alcoholics who developed their own circles had become disenchanted with the Buchmanites. They felt that Buchman's four "Absolutes" seemed too rigid. The alcoholics disliked Buchman's emphasis upon the social elite instead of common folks. They eschewed the publicity that attended Buchman's movement; the alcoholics preferred anonymity. Thus, the alcoholics parted company with the followers of Frank Buchman; the separation was acrimonious.

Perhaps you have heard of the Buchmanites by another name: the Oxford Group. Maybe you are familiar with the names of some of the men who left the Buchmanites: Bill Wilson and Dr. Bob Smith. Perhaps you are acquainted with the group that spun off from the Buchmanites: Alcoholics Anonymous.

Frank Buchman himself was accused in 1936 of being sympathetic to Hitler.[14] Whether or not the charge was justifiable, the popularity of Buchman's movement declined in the years before the Second World War. Buchman viewed the subsequent rise of A.A. with contempt. For that matter, the leadership of A.A. refused to acknowledge their indebtedness to Frank Buchman until after his death in 1961.[15]

Even so, many of the principles and Steps of A.A. are derived from the angry Lutheran minister who sought to recreate the church.

An Unsettling Thought

Back in 1990, a pair of researchers named Shedler and Block published a long-term study about adolescent experimentation with marijuana and other drugs. These researchers concluded that a certain amount of dabbling with such forbidden substances was quite normal for teenagers, and that it did not necessarily mean that the young people were headed for lives of addiction or ruin. In fact, the researchers even suggested that the youth who did try some of these "controlled substances" were better adjusted emotionally in later life than people who had never done any such experimenting in their youth.

I find these conclusions disturbing. I believe that these researchers are saying that it is healthier to have sampled drugs or alcohol during adolescence than never to have tried them at all.

As the father of a teenager and a pre-teenager, I am troubled by the findings of this study. I have cautioned my sons many times about the perils of alcohol and drugs—so often that they roll their eyes whenever I begin to rehearse my speech. I worry about their future when I hear stories about the oceans of alcohol that are consumed on college campuses, and I voice my concerns to my sons regularly. Often, I have given my sons a nice, concise sermonette about avoiding alcohol and drugs—but these researchers have complicated the issue.

Perhaps another reason that I am unsettled by the findings of this study is the fact that I myself never did any experimenting with alcohol or drugs in my younger years. (I am not boasting about this, you understand. I am merely stating the truth.) In high school and college, I hung around with guys who enjoyed basketball, went to movies, and played "Spoons" (you know, the mindless card game), but we did not get involved with alcohol or drugs.

I have learned what I know about alcohol and drugs vicariously—not first-hand. I remember a patient I met in a

15

treatment center who told me about his penchant for drinking and brawling. "Do you know what it is like when you get really drunk, and then pick out the biggest guy in the bar to fight?" he asked me. "Do you know what I mean?" I had to confess that I did not know what he meant—not from personal experience—but I was listening to him.

I always have considered myself an odd sort of fellow. Maybe this is because I did not experiment with enough contraband in my youth—or, maybe it was my congenital eccentricity that kept me away from such things in the first place. Whatever the case, I do not begrudge other people their use of alcohol, as long as they do not abuse it. I do view underage drinking as the abuse of alcohol, by the way, which is why I plan to continue to remind my sons about the dangers of alcohol and drugs—adolescent developmental studies notwithstanding.

When Lewis and Clark made their famous journey across the North American continent, so I have read, they distributed whiskey to the Native Americans they encountered along the way. For some of these Native Americans, surely it was their first exposure to liquor. One of the tribes, the Arikaras, declined the offer of alcohol, however. Clark remembers the Arikaras in his journal: "They say we are no friends or we would not give them what makes them fools."[16]

You can have the findings of Shedler and Block. I will go with the wisdom of the Arikaras.

Anonymity

"Anonymity is the spiritual foundation of all our traditions..."
(Tradition 12)

In the mid-1980's, I had a conversation with a man who served as a missionary in Papua New Guinea. He told me about the explosion of alcohol abuse in that country. This man, who was a counselor by trade, had been commissioned to work in the area of alcohol awareness in Papua New Guinea.

This missionary would travel from one remote village to another, articulating the dangers which attend the misuse of alcohol. He said that the natives would listen quietly to his presentation, and sometimes ask questions. Frequently, they inquired what the initials "A.A." meant. The missionary had a difficult time answering this particular query, however, because the people of Papua New Guinea could not grasp what he meant by the word "anonymous." Apparently, the concept had no counterpart in their culture. In the rural areas of Papua New Guinea, the natives tend to be related to one another. They generally seem to know each other's business, too. Few secrets are possible in these isolated villages where many of the huts do not even have doors. The missionary found he could not explain the principle of anonymity to them, so he gave up, and replied that "A.A." simply stands for "Avoid Alcohol."

This explanation seemed to satisfy them.

You might be amused by the tale of a community so far out in the sticks that it cannot conceive of anonymity—but the truth is that anonymity is downright scarce in the rural areas in *our* country, too. Someone once observed that there is no anonymity in towns of less than 5,000 people.

Anonymity is the cornerstone of the A.A. program, and yet, many people in rural areas resist A.A. because they realize that everyone in town will know whose car was parked in front of the Catholic parish hall on Thursday night.

17

Rurality and anonymity have a hard time coexisting. I wonder whether city folks like Bill W. and Dr. Bob ever understood this problem.

I think that people in rural areas tend to get careless about anonymity. I know some solid members of A.A. and Al-Anon who think nothing of dropping the names of people who attended a meeting the previous night. It is not just the natives of Papua New Guinea who have a hard time with anonymity.

So, what does the word "anonymous" mean within the context of the Alcoholics Anonymous program?

1) Some say that anonymity means that no one reveals who goes to A.A. meetings or what is discussed there. A sign that frequently is displayed at A.A. meetings offers this terse reminder: "Whom you see here, what you hear here, when you leave here, let it stay here." Period.

2) There is also a less rigid interpretation of anonymity. Some claim that anonymity means that you never associate an A.A. story with a name, or allow the two to be connected in any way. According to this thinking, you can discuss what was said at a meeting, as long as you keep the focus on "principles, not personalities" (to draw upon the vocabulary of the second half of Tradition 12).

3) Maybe anonymity means not using last names at meetings. Some people at A.A. meetings even refuse to divulge where they live or work.

4) By some accounts, anonymity means not trumpeting your name and the story of your recovery before the news media (as Tradition 11 would recommend).

Personally, I think we can either be too lax or too strict about anonymity. For the record, I believe that the founders of A.A. were interested in protecting recovering alcoholics from exposure to the press, not creating a circle of secrecy.[17] Dr. Bob warned against being so anonymous that others cannot reach you for help.[18]

I think that there is no excuse for naming people who attended the A.A. meeting the other night. Anonymity is hard to come by in rural areas, but there is one gesture that would speak clearly to anyone, from any culture, who blabs about who said what at an A.A. meeting.

It involves a boot—or, in Papua New Guinea, a swift sandal (figuratively speaking, of course).

Be Sly

An older man once told me a tale of his youth. The man said that he had been raised on a farm by his parents. (He had had some brothers, but they were considerably older than he; his brothers had moved away from home while he was still a youngster.) When this man was about 12, he wished that he could drive the family car. It was a '23 Dodge, he recalled. He knew in his heart that he could handle the car all by himself, but he was afraid to ask for permission.

One afternoon when his parents were not at home, he could not contain his desire any longer. He made up his mind that he was going to drive that car. He fired up the automobile, backed it out of the garage, and took it for a spin around the yard. He guided the car in a circle, about 25 times, and then eased the Dodge back into the garage, basking in triumph.

When he glanced out at the yard, however, he realized that he had left a ring of tire tracks in the dirt. He was certain that his parents would notice the tracks when they returned home, so he formulated a plan. He went out to the barn and fetched some cracked corn. Then he fed the chickens in a wide circle on the yard. He was hoping that the chicken scratches would obscure the tire tracks in the dirt. The ruse worked. His parents never did find out about his brief joyride.

As the man recalled this incident, he chuckled to himself, and uttered a phrase in a language I did not understand. It was a Low German proverb, he explained. With an impish grin on his face, he translated for me: "Be sly. Everyone is smart."

A lot of people are intelligent, this proverb would suggest. Sometimes, however, you may need to be *shrewd* in order to get what you want.

I remember a time when I applied for a job, and did not get it. When I told a co-worker about how the interview had gone, she rebuked me. "You're too darned honest," she scolded.

I was taken aback. Until that moment, I had never thought of honesty as anything but a virtue. Do you mean to say that even honesty can be a character defect? I began to wonder if some of what I had considered honesty was really naiveté. How did that Low German proverb go again? *Be sly. Everyone is smart.*

Normally, the 12-Step program advocates honesty and openness. A.A. usually counsels candor, not guile or duplicity. Chemical dependency often is described as a *cunning* disease. Some alcoholics claim they can hear an inner voice called "Slick" which urges them, "Be sneaky. Be clever. No one will ever know." Ordinarily, recovery is about resisting Old Slick, and being truthful and forthright instead.

Honesty is a requirement for recovery, and yet, there is also something to be said for cunning. I am not endorsing deceitfulness—like the 12-year-old who helped himself to the family car, and then literally had to cover his tracks—but I am suggesting that in some instances it might be a good thing to be cagey or crafty or canny or calculating. Sometimes, you might need to be clever in order to make "the system" work for you, in order to advance your own self-interests, or in order to get what you want. *Be sly! Everyone is smart!*

As I recall the early history of the A.A. movement, Bill W. and some other alcoholics broke away from the Oxford Group and formed their own Alcoholics Anonymous group, in part, because they were not comfortable with the emphasis the Oxford Group placed upon *Absolute* Honesty.[19] Honesty is a good thing, generally speaking, but *Absolute Honesty* is another matter. Absolute Honesty leaves no room for personal strategy or selective self-disclosure.

If it is not enough to enlist the support of Bill W., how about Jesus of Nazareth? What exactly did Jesus mean when he cautioned (in Matthew 10:16), "Be wise as serpents and innocent as doves"? What does it mean to be both wise and innocent at the same time?

Be sly...

Bill W.? A Ladies' Man?

An acquaintance of mine once made the remark that Bill Wilson was not only a married man, but also a "ladies' man." When I inquired what he meant by this, the fellow chuckled and replied, "Old Bill had his dollies on the side." He claimed that the guys talked about it at A.A. meetings now and then.

At the time, I did not place much store in this fellow's words. Bill W. literally wrote the book on Alcoholics Anonymous, for crying out loud! It is a program that requires rigorous honesty of its adherents.

How could one of the founding fathers of A.A. hang on to his own sobriety—much less blaze a trail to better living for millions of other alcoholics to follow—if he made a practice of pursuing "forbidden" relationships with women other than his wife? Please. Let's give Bill W. credit for having a little more integrity than this.

I scoffed at the notion that Bill W. was a "womanizer" in his sober years...until I heard a speaker at a workshop make the very same claim.

The speaker made reference to a book by Nan Robertson called *Getting Better: Inside Alcoholics Anonymous* (a Pulitzer Prize winner, by the way). I purchased a copy of this book and read it. The book delves into the history of A.A., and does provide further information about the claim that Bill W. was involved romantically with women other than his wife: ". . . Bill Wilson was a compulsive womanizer. His flirtations and his adulterous behavior filled him with guilt, according to old-timers close to him, but he continued to stray off the reservation."[20]

The author of this book observes that Bill W. stipulated in his will that some of the royalties from the Big Book would go to his wife and some to his paramour: ". . . 13.5 percent of the books' retail price for Lois and 1.5 percent for Helen W., Bill's last and most enduring mistress."[21]

This written testimony to Wilson's extramarital relationships was disturbing to me. Bill W.? The one who pioneered the way to sobriety? A woman-chaser?

These days, it has become almost commonplace to read about the sexual dalliances of famous figures. I am no longer fazed by stories about the extramarital affairs of men like Bill Clinton, John Kennedy, and Franklin Roosevelt. I am only slightly ruffled by similar rumors about Martin Luther King.

The notion that Bill W. was a philanderer throughout his married life, however, stirred something deep within me. I believe it was a sense of betrayal.

Perhaps I am naive about these things, but I had always given Bill W. more credit than to "fool around" behind his wife's back. The man advocated a spiritual program for recovery—involving fierce honesty and openness—and yet, it seems that he himself carried on with the ladies. How can this be?

I have known a good many alcoholics who have come to terms with their addiction to alcohol, but not their sexual overdrive. Although these people have learned to say "no" to alcohol in their lives, they have not learned to place any limits on their sexual overtures and behaviors—and it generally leads them into trouble, and from there, back to drinking. In fact, there is a saying in A.A. that goes like this: "Under every skirt, there is a slip."

All of this leads back to the question of how Bill W. could keep his own sobriety when he could not keep his wedding vows, and the larger question of how this guy could lay the cornerstone for the A.A. movement when he himself could not deal squarely with his own wife. Bill W.? A "womanizer"? Say it isn't so!

After turning these questions over in my mind for a while, I guess that I have made peace with Bill W. and his alleged sexual issues. I have moved from *disbelief* to *indignation* to *acceptance*.

Somebody once observed that "the vices of great men are usually on the same scale as their virtues."[22] On the surface, this

23

statement smacks of rationalization, and yet, there might be something to it.

It occurs to me that some of the greatest heroes in the Bible were also scandalous characters. Abraham offered his own wife to some other men just to save his own skin; Jacob cheated his own flesh and blood; Moses was a murderer; King David was an adulterer.

And then there was Bill W.

Bill W. may have helped start the A.A. program, but he was not an ideal human being. His character was flawed. So is yours and mine. Bill W. was not a person to be emulated in every way, but he was a man steeped in integrity, nevertheless, who pointed the way to sobriety. He had a scandalous side as well as a spiritual side, it seems.

The *Twenty-Four Hours a Day* book offers this reminder: "We should remember that all A.A.'s have 'clay feet.' We should not set any member upon a pedestal and mark her or him out as a perfect A.A. ... A.A. itself should be our ideal, not any particular member of it."[23]

So much for the matter of Bill Wilson's marital infidelity. Now then, have you heard that Bill W. encouraged experimentation with LSD as a substitute for alcohol?[24] No, I'm not kidding.

Boredom

A young man sat in my office at an addictions treatment center. He was laboring to explain the circumstances that led to his problem with alcohol. Finally, he gave up the struggle and sighed, "There is just nothing to do in a small town but drink." I nodded my head, as if to lend credence to his observation, but I knew that I had heard this line before.

Actually, it is a rather common complaint: there is nothing to do in rural communities except drink. I do not believe this is true, mind you, but it is a familiar grievance. I wanted to ask this young man, "Are there no books to read in your hometown? Is there no basketball hoop in your village? Are there no fish in proximity to the hamlet you call home?"

I think that what he meant to say was that, "There is nothing I want to do in my hometown but drink."

If this young man were to live in a metropolitan environment—where there are indoor tennis courts, professional baseball games, opera performances, and shopping galore—do you suppose he would keep himself so busy that he would no longer drink beer to excess? To put it another way, what do you suppose suburban teenagers do with their weekends, they who have so many entertaining options?

When this young man blamed his drinking on the monotony of his hometown, I dismissed it as an excuse.

That same afternoon, however, I spoke with another man in my office, this time a middle-aged fellow. He had gone through treatment about a year before, and had managed to stay sober for about nine months before he succumbed to relapse. He stated that there was no particular problem that prompted his return to drinking, just plain old boredom. The man allowed that he simply got tired of staring at his television, so he ambled downtown to the bar. He sounded credible, too.

When the younger man attributed his drinking to the lack of excitement in his hometown, it sounded like an excuse—but

25

when the second man blamed his drinking on his boredom, it seemed authentic. I do not believe that people drink because life in a small town is inherently boring, but I would believe that people might drink because their lives are boring.

Boredom is a spiritual issue, not just for alcoholics, but for a lot of other people, as well.

I grew up on a farm, 12 miles from the nearest town. I recall feeling restless, at times, during summer vacations and Christmas vacations. Whenever I would complain of boredom to my mother, she would proceed to list some things I could do, some of them work, some of them play. No matter how many suggestions she would offer, however, none ever seemed like the solution to my tedium. In retrospect, I think I was missing my friends from school, even though I expressed my discontent in terms of being *bored*. Maybe it is easier to admit to boredom than loneliness. I believe that boredom is not so much a matter of having nothing to do as it is a feeling of being disconnected. The feeling of boredom says more about *isolation* than it does about a need for *action, excitement, and adventure*. In short, boredom is not the opposite of staying *busy*, but the opposite of *relationship*.

Boredom is a spiritual issue. Bars and casinos tend to cater to bored people—but, in the end, bars are lonely places, and gambling is not entertaining enough to fill the void called boredom. An author by the name of Henri Nouwen once mused: "The great paradox of our time is that many of us are busy and bored at the same time."[25]

Boredom is a strain of loneliness. It is the need to have meaningful ties to others. It is the deep desire to be known by God, or by other people. To some degree, boredom is a part of everyone's life. Everybody needs to get into a car sometimes and drive away in search of a weekend adventure. A temporary change of scenery might very well be the antidote to common boredom, too—but chronic boredom is something else. It is a relational need. It is a spiritual issue.

I still do not believe that there is nothing to do in a small town except drink, but I am convinced that boredom is a widespread problem, in great cities and small towns alike.

There are various ways to contend with boredom—drinking, gambling, or keeping busy are some of them—but boredom is, in the end, a relational deficiency. It is a spiritual issue.

Let the *Twenty-Four Hours a Day* meditation book have the final word on the subject: "Nobody's bored at an A.A. meeting."[26]

Can a Person be a Higher Power?

I once had a conversation with a pastor who mentioned that he did not like the way they talk about a *Higher Power* in the Alcoholics Anonymous program. It bothered him that they did not use the word *God*. He told me that he had even heard of a guy who claimed that his next-door-neighbor was his Higher Power—which struck this pastor as something ludicrous.

Is it true that A.A. members sometimes speak of other people as their Higher Power?

Allow me to set forth in writing the response I made to this pastor.

Many people who are chemically dependent seem to have a hard time with religion in general, and with the term *God* in particular. Some have endured a grave loss or a wound during their life, for which they blame God. Many alcoholics struggle with authority, which the word *God* might represent to them. The disease of chemical dependency itself can choke off a person's spiritual sensitivities, and make any talk of God seem repugnant.

Whatever their reasons, many alcoholics have an adverse reaction to the word God—either because it suggests something negative to them, or because it does not seem to mean anything at all.

The A.A. program maintains that chemically dependent people do need some help from outside of themselves in order to achieve sobriety. In order to circumvent the stigma that may surround the word God, A.A. people frequently employ a phrase with a neutral connotation: *Higher Power*. It is a basic premise in A.A. that everyone has a sacred right to construe a Higher Power in any way that makes sense to that individual person.

If someone protests at an A.A. meeting, "I don't believe in God!"—that person might be encouraged to find a different way to conceive of a Higher Power. "You can, if you wish, make A.A. itself your 'higher power,'" writes Bill Wilson.[27] This is not to equate A.A. with God, but merely to make the point that there is an abundance of positive energy in a room whenever alcoholics are gathered to support one another.

If you cannot bring yourself to believe in God, in other words, you might seek help from some other people who seem trustworthy. "For thousands of members," Bill W. notes, "the A.A. group itself has been a 'Higher Power' in the beginning."[28]

Some alcoholics who have difficulty with the notion of God may choose to think of their Higher Power as their A.A. sponsor. This, of course, is not to say that they are designating their A.A. sponsor as some sort of divine figure. It simply means that they are willing to accept some care and guidance from another human being. It means that they are starting somewhere to learn to trust.

There is a risk involved in defining your Higher Power in terms of another person. (What if your A.A. sponsor steers you wrong? What if your A.A. sponsor goes back to drinking?) It probably is safer to think of an A.A. group as a Higher Power instead of an individual, but either option, hopefully, represents an attempt at trust, which is necessary for recovery.

Bill W. himself was aware of the liabilities inherent in construing a group or a person as a Higher Power, and yet, he remarks, "We should all be glad that good recoveries can be made even on this limited basis."[29] Some people eventually come to the conclusion that it is not enough to think of a Higher Power in terms of other people. Others, however, remain content with this way of thinking.

It is true that A.A. people sometimes use the expression *Higher Power* instead of the word *God*. This substitution is not intended to be something sacrilegious, but rather a way for some alcoholics to get beyond their negative reaction to the term *God*. It is also true that some A.A. members will conceptualize their Higher Power in terms of other people, but this is not about perverting theology. It is about learning to trust.

Coffee

An A.A. member once told me about his vacation travels, which had taken him through Akron, Ohio—the home of Dr. Bob and Anne Smith. While in Akron, this A.A. member had toured the Smith's home, which has been turned into a museum. There the man saw a replica of Anne Smith's famous coffeepot. (The Smiths' actual coffeepot is in the possession of their daughter.)

The fellow who shared this tale with me is not an especially sentimental sort, but he confessed that he had become misty-eyed as he stood gazing at that old pot. He said that he was touched by the realization that Anne had poured coffee from a vessel very much like this one to Bob and Bill at the kitchen table, as the two shared their struggles with alcoholism with one another, thereby laying the foundation for the A.A. program.

It is a symbol of the A.A. fellowship, that old pot. Who could say how many suffering people had gathered around just such a coffeepot in Anne and Bob's home in the early days? They came to talk about their troubles, and to sip the brew of Anne's coffeepot. It is said that if A.A. has a sacred relic, it must be Anne Smith's coffeepot.

To this day, coffee-drinking and A.A. seem to go together. Recovery is something that happens when alcoholics begin to talk over their cups of coffee. "As anonymous members have put it at unrecorded times: 'All you need to start a new group is a resentment and a coffeepot.'"[30] For some reason, coffee tends to be an important element in the recovery process.

So, what is the deal with coffee? There definitely is some kind of mystique about this common black substance. Some say that coffee is even the *sacrament* of A.A. It is a catalyst, of sorts. It makes something happen. It helps people transcend their differences. Coffee seems to bring people together, with their defenses lowered. Is there actually some healing quality about coffee, or is it just a hot beverage that happens to go well with gentle conversation?

I think that coffee-drinking provides an excuse for people to be together. Drinking coffee is more than a simple act in itself; it is a social activity. One suggests, "Let's go get a cup of coffee" in the same spirit that one would propose, "Let's go have a beer" or, "Let's go smoke a cigarette." It just does not sound the same, however, to suggest, "Let's go get some pop" or, "Let's go eat some apples."

Drinking coffee connotes socializing, hanging out, or "schmoozing." The caffeine in coffee—like the nicotine in cigarettes, or the ethyl alcohol in beer—seems to smooth the way for social interaction. For some reason, addictive substances (like coffee) seem to make effective social lubricants.

I myself do not drink coffee, and I never have. It is not easy, let me tell you, being a Norwegian and a Lutheran and a minister—and yet not a consumer of coffee. My father used to pour coffee into a saucer to cool it, and then slurp it right out of the saucer, but I myself have never been a coffee-drinker. Many times I have been asked why I do not drink coffee, but I simply do not know. I am sure I would be a better schmoozer if I did wrap my hand around a coffee mug and partake—but I have never had a yen for it.

Sometimes I tell people that I do not drink coffee because I have heard so many stories about all of those dogs that run free in the bean fields in Columbia, but this is an excuse. I really do not know why I do not drink coffee.

My favorite drug has always been *resentment*. While my co-workers take breaks to indulge in their coffee or cigarettes, I kick back and think bitter thoughts about my boyhood, being a benchwarmer in basketball, and things like that. Let the others have their coffee, but make mine a tall glass of bile.

I do not intend to learn to drink coffee anytime soon, either. In fact, there is only one way that I would ever consent to consume a cup of coffee: if it were served out of Anne Smith's own pot.

Gregory P. Gabriel

Coincidences

"When I pray, coincidences happen;
when I stop praying, the coincidences stop happening."
(William Temple[31])

I remember an occasion when an attractive young woman came to treatment for her chemical dependency. She was a flirtatious sort. Whenever she was in the company of males, she became especially animated and entertaining.

On the day after her arrival at treatment, another young woman entered the treatment program, and was assigned to be her roommate. This second woman was both pretty and coquettish in her own right. The two took an immediate dislike to one another, to put it mildly. The first woman called her counterpart "a Barbie doll in cowboy boots." The other responded with an epithet I shall not bother to specify.

A counselor helped these women to sort through their mutual animosity. Each of the women complained about the way the other would "bat her eyes" around menfolk. Through their conversation, however, each woman realized that what she did not like about the other woman was what she did not like about herself.

Was it an accident—merely an accident—that these two women with such obvious similarities arrived at treatment at virtually the same time, and were asked to share the same living quarters? It may not have been a monumental coincidence, but it seemed to be a meaningful coincidence, at least in the sense that it served to open both of their eyes.

A.A. members have a saying about coincidences like the one I have just described: "Coincidences are God's way of preserving his anonymity." According to A.A. thinking, one of the ways that a Higher Power works from behind the scenes is to bring two corresponding events (or people) into the same place and time.

In other words, one way to discern the hand of God is to look for meaningful coincidences. The practice of paying attention to coincidences can fall into abuse—obviously, not all coincidences are significant ones—and yet, a great many A.A. members seem to chart the story of their recovery by reference to some of the coincidences they have experienced along the way. I am reminded of a patient in a chemical dependency treatment program who, after listening to a peer discuss some of his drinking history, remarked, "I feel like I just met myself walking down the street."

A lot of coincidences seem to occur in treatment programs and at A.A. meetings.

There is a technical term for a coincidence: "synchronicity." This word is attributed to Dr. Carl Jung, an eminent Swiss psychiatrist (with whom Bill W. corresponded). The term "synchronicity" can be broken down to "syn" (which means "same") and "chronicity" (which relates to the word "chronos" or "time"). Jung not only explored the significance of events that happen at the "same time," but also stressed that an alcoholic is going to require some spiritual assistance in order to maintain sobriety.

A.A. has always treasured both of these Jungian thoughts, and perhaps even joined them together. Many recovering alcoholics seek spiritual insight in the coincidences of their lives.

Some coincidences are relatively modest—like the two flirtatious women who found themselves roommates at a treatment center—but others are downright dramatic. There is an intriguing story in a book called *Came to Believe*[32] about a recovering alcoholic who lived in Wisconsin, and sometimes did some speaking at A.A. meetings in his area. The man encountered some hard times, and decided to go back to drinking. He planned to drive to Chicago, where no one would know him, and get drunk. Although there were many thousands of bars in Chicago, he happened to walk into one that was staffed by a bartender who had once heard him give his A.A. talk.

It was a remarkable coincidence. The man did not return to drinking after all. Through this stroke of synchronicity, his Higher Power had spoken to him only too clearly.

Compulsive Gambling and Sex

A man once came to a treatment center for an assessment to determine whether he was a compulsive gambler. He was accompanied by his concerned spouse. When the assessment process indicated that he did indeed have an addiction to gambling, his wife was greatly relieved. She had been afraid that he had been having an affair with another woman. What else could explain his strange behavior—his absences in the evenings, his way of sneaking around, and his evasiveness when questioned? When she learned that the core problem was compulsive gambling, she was so happy that she wept tears of joy. She had been worried that she had lost him entirely, but the root problem was his obsession with gambling.

This anecdote might seem slightly amusing to you, but it also points to some deeper truths about the problem of compulsive gambling. Many people do not appreciate how serious compulsive gambling can be, or how profoundly it can affect a person. The concerned wife was naïve about compulsive gambling if she automatically assumed it is a lesser problem than infidelity.

It is interesting that she mistook the problem of compulsive gambling for adultery. There is something distinctly sexual about the problem of compulsive gambling. I have heard compulsive gamblers say things like, "I was having an affair with a slot machine," or, "My gambling was my mistress." Sometimes compulsive gamblers describe the allure of gambling as something downright seductive. There does seem to be some kind of an affinity between compulsive gambling and sex. It is not difficult to believe that a woman could confuse the issue of compulsive gambling with unfaithfulness on the part of her husband.

Consider these points of correlation between compulsive gambling and various sexual issues:

❑ Many people who come to treatment for compulsive gambling are victims of sexual abuse. Is there some connection between the painful memories of sexual abuse and the comfort derived from gambling?

❑ Many compulsive gamblers use sex as a means of manipulation— either to put a spouse in a frame of mind that would be amenable to going gambling that evening, or else to help a spouse to forgive and forget gambling losses. Of all the ways a compulsive gambler could seek to control a spouse, why is sex such a common tool?

❑ One compulsive gambler acknowledged that whenever he lost large sums of money at a casino, he would go into a restroom and masturbate because he desperately needed "some way to feel good." What is the link between the thrill of gambling and self-stimulation?

❑ Once compulsive gamblers cease to gamble, they seem to be at risk of falling into sexual addiction—including preoccupation with sex, extremely promiscuous behavior, or engrossment in pornography. How come it is so easy for compulsive gamblers to substitute sexual addiction for their gambling habit?

I do not think of myself as an authority on the subject of compulsive gambling (or sex), but I once heard a medical expert make the assertion that compulsive gambling seems to arouse the same part of the brain that is stimulated by sex. One cannot help but wonder about the similarities between the two.

Coping With Christmas

Some people hate Christmas...

Everyone knows that the yuletide is supposed to be a joyful time, a season for singing and cheer, gift-giving and warm family gatherings. For some folks, however, it is an especially painful portion of the calendar. There are many reasons why people might dread Christmas, but a very common one has to do with family relationships. Those who are dissatisfied with their families throughout the year sometimes feel keenly unhappy at the holidays, when it seems as though everyone else is reveling in the glow of family get-togethers.

Alcoholism has a way of straining and breaking relationships. It can create friction, or perhaps distance, within family systems. When Christmas rolls around again, many who have lived in homes afflicted by alcoholism feel particularly alienated, frustrated, depressed, or even suicidal.

It is an ancient problem: holidays which bring family pain to the fore. There are, however, some classic suggestions about how to cope with the distress that sometimes attends Christmas. The counsel might be placed in three categories: 1) Al-Anon's Advice; 2) the Counselor's Cure; and 3) the Preacher's Perspective.

1) Al-Anon's Advice: The Al-Anon program advocates lowering one's expectations of family, especially at the holidays. According to this line of reasoning, the problem is not so much one's sorry excuse for a family as it is one's lofty expectations of what family should be. The solution is to adopt realistic expectations of one's relatives. If your unaffectionate father has never, in 40 years, put his arms around you and told you that you have been a good son or daughter, why should you hope to hear these words from him this Christmas?

Instead of anticipating a cozy and satisfying Christmas Eve with your (sorely dysfunctional?) family, could you settle for something less than your ideal? Rather than looking forward to a *great* Christmas with your kinsfolk (and thereby setting yourself up for frustration if your dream is not realized) might you think in terms of having an *okay* Christmas with them?

Could you aim to exchange Christmas pleasantries with relatives without warring? Might you attempt to have a meal with your family without rancor? Would that be enough of a Christmas for you, or do you insist upon something more? Could you watch a football game or a Christmas special on television, in the presence of your relatives, and find it minimally fulfilling?

If you cannot have an *okay* Christmas with your family members, it is probably wisest not to meet with them at all. There is no reason to get together with your relatives if you feel nothing but misery in their company. If you do find *some* satisfaction in being with your family, though, let it be enough. Al-Anon's advice is to lower your expectations of your family at the holidays.

2) The Counselor's Cure: I once heard a psychologist remark that many people chafe at Christmas time because they simply do not know "how to bring Santa Claus." That is, they do not know how to delight themselves (or, in the jargon of therapists, "the child within"). Some people keep waiting for their family, or anyone else, to do something for them that would constitute Christmas. They do not know how to give themselves what they really want or need. Perhaps you will have to get your affirmation from somewhere other than your biological family (from an A.A. or Al-Anon group?) or maybe you will have to give the gift to yourself. For those who hate Christmas, it is the Counselor's Cure.

3) The Preacher's Perspective: The church, too, has a word of advice for those who dislike the thought of Christmas: Advent. In the Christian tradition, the four weeks before Christmas are not devoted to celebrating, much less loathing to celebrate with family members. Advent is all about lighting a candle and sitting quietly before that small flame—allowing yourself to hope and wonder what the coming Christmas might bring. Who knows but that one might find in the flicker of the candle what he or she fears cannot be found at the Christmas gathering with the relatives.

   In the words of an old Christmas hymn, "The hopes and fears of all the years are met in thee tonight."

Gregory P. Gabriel

Courtesy

"Of Courtesy: it is much less
Than courage of heart or holiness.
Yet in my walks it seems to me
That the grace of God is in Courtesy."
(Hilaire Belloc: "Courtesy")

I have no idea who Hilaire Belloc might be, but this ditty about courtesy is cited in the *One Day at a Time in Al-Anon* book.[33] The last line of the poem is especially intriguing to me: *The grace of God is in courtesy.*

Now, *grace* sounds like something noble or profound. A working definition for *grace* might be when you are treated far better than you have a right to expect. Grace is something sublime.

Courtesy, on the other hand, is something common. Courtesy is nothing more than treating other people with respect.

This poem brings together the sublime and the ordinary: the grace of God is in courtesy. To re-work the sentence slightly, perhaps it suggests that if there is evidence of the grace of God, it may well be found in common courtesy.

I think that simple courtesy is somewhere near the heart of what goes on at a treatment center. When you get right down to it, recovery is deeply intertwined with civility and kindness and even good manners.

I believe that the patients who come to treatment for their addictions are treated with dignity and hospitality. In the sense that others listen to them, they are shown great courtesy. Insofar as they are treated as people who are ill, instead of people who are bad, they are shown due respect.

The patients at a treatment center are expected to show consideration for others, too. They are expected to wait patiently in the lunch line, instead of barging to the fore. They are expected not to "ogle" other people in a lustful way. They are urged to listen to other people without interrupting. They are

40

urged not to belch loudly or use language laced with vulgarities. When they receive a compliment, they are enjoined simply to say "thank you," instead of discounting it.

Recovery does have something to do with decorum and treating other people respectfully. The grace of God is in courtesy.

I remember a woman who told me about her childhood in an alcoholic household. She claimed that her family rarely had any guests in her home because her father, who was an alcoholic, treated people so rudely. Her father did not forbid friends or relatives to enter their house, she recalled, but if they did come, he spoke to them with sarcasm or outright contempt, so they were not inclined to come again.

Alcoholism is a rude disease. It exerts an influence over people that is crude and forceful.

This may sound odd, but one way to cope with someone else's chemical dependency is with courtesy. The family members of an alcoholic can learn in Al-Anon how to respond to the disease with carefully measured words and with restraint, indeed, with politeness. When family members scold and threaten and scream at a chemically dependent person, no good purpose is served.

When family members employ tact and patience and empathy—which are all expressions of courtesy—they make room for the chemically dependent person to respond in kind. It simply is not respectful to make a decision for another human being. When family members of an alcoholic begin to "remember their manners," some positive things can happen in their relationship with the alcoholic.

It all starts with courtesy.

Obviously, courtesy alone is not the answer to the problem of chemical dependency, but is an important part of the solution. The grace of God tends to show up in the little things, like the ways in which people talk to one another. Spirituality is when the noble is found in the commonplace.

If there is evidence of the grace of God, perhaps it is manifest in common courtesy.

Divine Dissatisfaction

It was a frigid night in New York City during the winter of 1940. The rain had turned to sleet. Bill W. and his wife were living in the A.A. clubhouse on 24th Street. They had been put out of their house, and forced to take refuge in a dreary bedroom in the upstairs of the clubhouse.

It was a low point in Bill's life. Although he had not taken a drink in six years, Bill was feeling deeply discouraged. He was unemployed. The A.A. program was not developing as he thought it would. Some of his friends in the program had drifted back to drinking. The Big Book he had authored was not selling very well. He had been criticized for his leadership of A.A.; some even accused him of trying to make a profit from the program. Bill was feeling misunderstood and unappreciated.[34]

He was angry about his circumstances. He was filled with self-pity. Surely, his living arrangements did nothing to lift his spirits.

The doorbell rang at about 10 o'clock that night. (His wife was not at home at the time.) The janitor came upstairs to inform Bill that a "bum" from St. Louis was asking to talk to Bill, like many other alcoholics who came to him to pour out their troubles. Despite his wintry mood, Bill consented to see the man.

Presently, a short, white-haired man limped into Bill's tiny bedroom. He walked with the assistance of a cane. The man's coat was dripping wet. He settled into a chair, and began to loosen his coat. As the man opened his raincoat, Bill realized that his visitor was wearing a clerical collar.

The older man was not a bum at all, but a Jesuit priest. His name was Father Ed Dowling, and he had indeed come from St. Louis. Father Dowling was an editor of a Catholic journal, and was interested in learning more about the A.A. program.

Father Dowling was intrigued by the similarities between the 12 Steps of A.A. and the Exercises of St. Ignatius (the spiritual principles of the Jesuit order). Father Dowling was amused when

Bill replied that he was not familiar with the Exercises of St. Ignatius.

This priest had a wise and gentle way about him. Bill soon came to feel very comfortable with this humble fellow. Bill began to describe some of his frustration and dejection, while Father Dowling listened intently. Bill shared deeply of himself that night. He later realized that he, unknowingly, had presented his Fifth Step to this complete stranger.

After Bill had detailed his anguish and unhappiness, Father Dowling responded with a quote from Matthew 5: "Blessed are they who do hunger and thirst." In essence, he blessed Bill's discontent. "God's chosen, he pointed out, were always distinguished by their yearnings, their restlessness, their thirst."[35]

Father Dowling described something he called "divine dissatisfaction"—something that spurs people onward, something that motivates them. The priest suggested that human yearning is something God can press into the service of his own will.

Bill asked whether there could ever be any relief for this restlessness and frustration. "Never," Father Dowling replied curtly. "Never any."[36]

"He continued in a gentler tone, describing as 'divine dissatisfaction' that which would keep [Bill W.] going, always reaching out for unattainable goals, for only by so reaching would he attain what—hidden from him—were God's goals."[37]

I suspect that all people share a secret dream that someone would come to them, listen to their complaints, help them to accept their unhappiness, and encourage them to keep striving. Father Ed Dowling—who served as a spiritual advisor to Bill W. over the next 20 years—helped Bill to understand the concept of "divine dissatisfaction."

Fancy Words and Lugubrious People

There I was. Walking down the hallway at my place of employment. Minding my own business. Wasn't bothering anybody. I was carrying a can of Diet Coke in my hand. Just minding my own business. Wasn't bothering anybody.

I cannot remember why I paused at the doorway of the staff dining room, but I did. It was around noon. That is when it happened. A female colleague called out to me from the dining room, "Is that your lunch?"

I glanced at the can of pop in my hand. Then I looked back at the woman who had put the question to me. "No," I replied innocently, "this is my beverage."

The woman let out a hoot of derision, followed by a malicious cackle. All eyes in the dining room turned to the woman who was tittering uncontrollably, and then toward me and my pop can.

"Your beverage?" she inquired, with a mannish guffaw. Clearly, she was amused by my choice of words. She was jiggling with mirth. It was an evil sort of glee.

She choked back her laughter enough to say, "Most people would call that a can of pop."

"I thought it was obvious that it was a can of pop," I offered in my own defense. "Most people are able to recognize a can of pop when they see one."

By this time, she was quaking in merriment. "His beverage!" she screeched. Then she emitted a snort, which broke up everyone in the dining room, except me.

"You asked me if this were my lunch," I explained calmly and matter-of-factly, "and I replied that it is my beverage."

The key word "beverage" touched off another fit of raucous laughter. I gathered that she thought I was being "uppity" or condescending when I used the "b-word." Evidently, she believed that I was "putting on airs."

45

Gregory P. Gabriel

(Now I ask you, good reader, is there anything wrong with using the word "beverage"? It's not a "hoity-toity" term, is it?)

"How long have you had this fear of big words?" I asked her, trying to be helpful. "And how did you get through your professional training without using three-syllable words?"

Anything I said only caused her and the others to giggle more violently, so I walked away with my beverage, shaking my head, as the vicious chortling echoed down the hallway.

As I think back on my repartee with my co-worker over the word "beverage," I have decided that I owe her an apology. By the word apology, I do not mean to suggest that "I'm sorry," but rather, in the classical sense of the word apology, that I intend to put forth a formal defense.

I submit that the A.A. program calls for a robust vocabulary. I'm sorry, but it's true. The 12-Step program requires a flourishing command of the English language. Want proof?

If you page through the Big Book (3rd ed.), you will find some fancy words like "maelstrom" (page 2) and "opined" (p. 331) and "contretemps" (p. 520) and "insouciance" (p. 556). If you thumb through the *Twelve Steps and Twelve Traditions*, you may come across some tangy terms like "rapacious" (p. 21) or "tosspot" (p. 78) or "topers" (p. 170). In *One Day at a Time in Al-Anon*, we encounter words such as "insoluble" (p. 221) and "servile" (p. 270) and "solicitous" (p. 332) and—my personal favorite—"lugubrious" (p. 11).

Now there is a sturdy fellow: lugubrious (*loo-GOO-bree-es*). Go ahead and say it out loud, if you want. Lugubrious! It means being "mournful to an excessive degree." It is not only a delicious word—lugubrious—but it is also Conference-approved! It is right there in the *ODAT* book!

Now, I do not really believe any of what I have just written about the A.A. program requiring a broad vocabulary, but I shall argue the case anyway the next time I see my feminine detractor in the staff dining room. I shall stand in the doorway of the staff dining room, with my beverage in hand, rattling off Conference-

46

approved polysyllabic terms until she seems appropriately lugubrious.

Well, maybe I will not do this after all. It is a pleasant fantasy, though. If a stout vocabulary is not necessary for recovery, maybe a sense of humor is.

Gregory P. Gabriel

Fear of Falling

I remember an afternoon when I brought Holy Communion to some "homebound" members of the congregation I was serving. In all, I visited four homes: three of them widows in their mid-80s, and one elderly couple.

One woman trembled the whole time I sat in her living room. Another had sold her stuffed chair because it reminded her too much of "him." One was confused, even about who her son was. A fourth lived alone in a farmhouse, and only turned on the television to watch the polka dancing on Saturday evenings.

Do you now what elderly folks worry about? For one thing, they are afraid of falling. The people I called upon spoke of their wariness of stairways, of "trick" ankles, of icy sidewalks, and in general, of the devastating effects of going down.

One recalled that she had slept in a recliner for seven weeks after she had fallen and broken her sternum. Another said that she was not afraid of getting hurt in a fall, but that she worried that she would not be able to get to her feet again. It all seemed so vivid when they described their fears of taking a tumble.

One thing these elderly people had in common was a fear of falling. They all had learned from cruel experience to conduct themselves with care, and they did not seem especially bitter about the lesson life had forced upon them, either. Somehow, they had learned to live gracefully—as well as fearfully—within new limits.

I suppose that this is essentially what brings people to Alcoholics Anonymous in the first place: the instinctive fear of falling. Have you noticed that much of the vocabulary in A.A. concerns things like *steps* and *slips* and *walking the walk* and *balance*? When a traffic cop stops a motorist on suspicion of drunken driving, the officer wants to see whether the driver is able to walk in a straight line without staggering. If a fitting metaphor for active alcoholism is the out-of-control stumbling—

48

then recovery is about gaining stable footing, and about acquiring a healthy fear of falling in the first place.

It might be observed that alcoholics are those who need to learn abruptly the lesson that life teaches everyone else over the years—that is, a sturdy respect for limits in general, and the severe fear of slipping in particular.

Experts on aging claim that growing older is not necessarily something negative (despite the premium our culture places on being youthful). While the aging process does bring physical decline, and with it the danger of falling, aging can also be accompanied by increased potential. In other words, the more one ages, the more one becomes aware of one's limits (so I am told) and the more one is inclined to accept the reality that "I-am-not-God."

It is a freeing thing for a person to realize that there are some things that he or she cannot do. Youth does not understand mortality, and all this blather about accepting limits, but the aged do. Senior citizens gradually learn to stay away from staircases in the same way that recovering alcoholics learn to avoid alcohol, or even the resentment that seems to justify a drink.

I suppose that it all comes down to the dread of pitching forward onto the ground.

Getting Too Close to the Drink

I used to live in a wee village in Nebraska, just a few miles south of the mighty Missouri River. Like any major river, the Missouri is a dangerous watercourse. Its waters run swift and strong. Old timers who live in the area agree that the river picked up speed after a dam was constructed to the west.

They say that there are some 40-foot drop-offs beneath those swirling waters. Every few years, some teenagers are bold enough to try swimming in the powerful currents, and they lose their lives in the churning river. Then entire towns grieve. Time and again, the villages along the Missouri learn the same cruel lesson.

The A.A. meetings in those parts are few and far between. As a matter of fact, the A.A. people typically meet with the Al-Anon folks, because they are so few. The average crowd at these joint meetings might be a foursome.

One such meeting had been under way for about 15 minutes on an evening in June when a disheveled-looking man of about 40 entered the room. He grinned shyly and pulled off his cap, but he remained standing. Some of the men at the meeting greeted him by name, although not everyone in the room knew him.

The man explained that he was a member of a team that had been dragging the river for the body of a boy who (it was well-known) had been swept away by the river a few days before. He produced a white card and requested, rather sheepishly, that someone sign it in order to substantiate his attendance at the A.A. meeting (presumably, to appease a probation officer somewhere).

Apparently, he wanted someone to endorse his card so that he could return to his grim search on the river. One of the men at the meeting made a faint attempt at humor, reached for the man's card, signed it, and handed it back to him. The man from the river smiled appreciatively, said thanks, and was gone.

The matter was settled just as quickly as it had arisen. Or was the matter settled? There seems to be something ironic about skipping an A.A. meeting to search for a dead body.

I am <u>not</u> suggesting that the man should have sat down at the meeting instead of returning to his grisly task at the river—although he might have accomplished more good by processing his experience at the meeting for 45 minutes than by hustling back to his boat. I am <u>not</u> saying that he belonged at the meeting instead of the river. I am certain that the victim's family was horribly traumatized by the loss, and that the recovery of the body was a matter of urgency for them.

Actually, it is none of my business whether the man stayed at the meeting or went back to the river. My point is that I would not have agreed to sign his card. If he had a legitimate reason to miss an A.A. meeting—and I think he did—he could have explained his absence to his probation officer himself. I, myself, would not have signed his card, though.

Perhaps my assessment of the situation seems severe, but I am of the opinion that a lot of people simply do not have enough respect for the power of alcohol. They underestimate the dangers which attend even casual drinking. Some lack a healthy fear of the disease of alcoholism. They venture too close to the drink.

The man from the river did not come back to the A.A. meeting in the weeks that followed. A lot of good people seem to get lost that way. Time and again, the villages along the Missouri learn the same cruel lessons. Sometimes, entire towns grieve.

Go Ahead and Call the Bishop

I work as a chaplain at a treatment center for chemically dependent people and compulsive gamblers.

This may sound odd, but I do not like to see patients who have a strong faith in God. I am suspicious of people who read the Bible while in treatment. And I cringe when patients ask to see me as the chaplain.

Permit me to explain.

Please do not write to my supervisor to complain about me, and do not call my Bishop either, at least not yet. Just hear me out.

A lot of people come to treatment with skewed ideas about God and religion and ministers. I suppose that part of my job is to help them untangle some of their thinking, but it is not easy sometimes.

Some who come to treatment assure me that their faith in God is steadfast. They tell me that they have always believed in God, that they pray every day, and that Jesus is their close, personal friend. "And He walks with me and He talks with me, and He tells me I am His own..."

The problem is this: I do not see how treatment can help people who do not need any help. I do not have anything to offer to someone who is already "tight" with God.

The treatment experience is a time when people examine their lives and their feelings and their relationships, including their relationship with God. Many people come to new conclusions about God while in treatment, which is harder to do if you boast that you have your faith-life "all together" from the moment you walk in the door. Some people have to de-construct their faith before they can fashion something new, something that will help to keep them sober or bet-free.

It is easier to work with a patient who does not have a clue about God than to deal with someone who professes to have all the answers. Frankly, I would rather contend with a card-carrying atheist than with someone who claims his or her faith-life is "just fine." At least an atheist knows where he or she stands.

I do not like it when people bring me their Bible puzzlers, either. Invariably, they want to dialogue about some cryptic verse in Ecclesiastes or Revelation. It usually works like this: first, they want to know if I think that Gog or Magog in Ezekiel could represent the former Soviet Union; next, I say something about them doing their written assignments honestly, and trusting their therapy group; then, they say something else about Gog and Magog.

One fellow sought me out to ask where in the Bible it says that God created the world 200 years ago. He told me he was pretty sure it was in the Old Testament. I replied that I did not know where this particular reference might be found. (I had always understood that the world was created before the American Revolution, not after it.)

The guy took a verbal swipe at me, which patients sometimes do when you do not tell them what they want to hear. This is the part I do not like about fielding theological inquiries: the part where I get my ears boxed.

There is a definite flow about the treatment process. The people who seem to get the program are those who learn to trust. When people ask to see a minister, it often means that they are fighting the current. I do get weary of meeting with self-styled spiritual seekers. You do not find spirituality by looking for it, anyway.

I guess that my job is to re-direct some of the errant questions that people present to me, but I do not like the "zingers" that come with this duty.

As I was saying, I do not like to see patients with a deep faith (read: "denial"). I do not like to see patients poring over their Bibles (in diversionary fashion). And, I am leery when patients ask to see me of their own accord (because I do not like to be cuffed).

Now, if you still want to complain about me to the Bishop, go ahead. While you have him on the phone, ask him if he thinks Gog or Magog could represent the former Soviet Union, too.

Guidance and Checking

When Bill W. first met Dr. Bob in Akron, Ohio in 1935, the two men discovered that they had much in common, from their respective boyhoods in Vermont to their struggles with alcoholism. They also realized that they both had been involved with the Oxford Group. When Bill W. and Dr. Bob discussed spiritual matters, they were able to converse in the terminology of the Oxford Group.

Maybe they even talked about *guidance* and *checking*—which were two technical terms from the vocabulary of the Oxford Group.

The members of the Oxford Group would meet in private homes, usually in groups of six to 12 people, to seek what they called *guidance*. They would sit in a circle, and begin their meetings with prayer—after which, they observed a long period of silence, perhaps even an hour, during which the participants would listen for directions from God.

The Oxford Group members sat with notebooks and pencils on their laps, ready to record whatever revelation might occur to them. Frequently, the messages that came to them were quite specific. One person might feel urged to give some money to a particular individual, or another could be instructed to go to a designated street corner and wait for a certain person to come along.

The adherents of the Oxford Group understood that not all guidance people claimed to have received actually came from God, so they practiced something called *checking*, which meant that one discussed with other people the ideas he or she believed had come from God, to see if others agreed that these ideas truly seemed divinely inspired. Sometimes, the validity of a person's guidance was judged by what were considered the "Four Absolutes" of the Oxford Group: Purity, Honesty, Unselfishness, and Love.

In the days before there was an A.A. program, some of the forefathers of A.A. practiced the ways of the Oxford Group, until they broke away and established groups specifically for alcoholics. Some of the alcoholics who took part in the Oxford Group objected to the emphasis upon *guidance*. Apparently, one could receive guidance on behalf of someone else, as in the time a woman informed Dr. Bob (whose sobriety was not yet secure) that she felt directed to tell him to give up drinking forever. Some of the alcoholics who sat in on Oxford Group sessions were uncomfortable with the practice of *checking*, as it sometimes became downright aggressive and confrontative. The alcoholics complained that the others were "taking their inventory." In the end, the alcoholics would not sit still for the long period of quiet which guidance required, or the criticism which checking sometimes entailed.

When Bill W. and Dr. Bob laid the foundation for the A.A. program, they drew from their experience in the Oxford Group, but they did not appropriate the specific methods called guidance and checking. Maybe they considered these techniques oppressive, or plainly naive. It does seem dangerously simplistic to believe that God will give you an *explicit* word of advice whenever you sit down to wait for it.

You will not find technical expressions like *guidance* and *checking* in the vocabulary of A.A.—but the same general principles are indeed part of the philosophy of A.A. today. A.A. certainly encourages people to be in conscious contact with a Higher Power, although this does not necessarily imply sitting quietly in a circle with a notebook in your lap.

You will not find technical terms such as "guidance" and "checking" in the literature of A.A., but you might find their imprint: "It is worth noting that people of very high spiritual development almost always insist on checking with friends or spiritual advisers the guidance they feel they have received from God."[38]

The specific customs of the Oxford Group, in a general way, are still alive in A.A. today.

Handwriting on the Wall

Once upon a time, there was a king named Belshazzar (whose story is recorded in the Book of Daniel, chapter 5). This king threw a boozy banquet for 1,000 of his closest friends. King Belshazzar and his guests were having a merry time, hoisting their goblets, praising their gods, and tossing back their wine.

Suddenly, this scene of mirth and revelry was shattered! Human fingers—not attached to any person—appeared near the wall! The fingers seemed to be writing something on the plaster. This was no hologram, but an honest-to-goodness hand scratching some sort of message on the wall.

Balshazzar was horrified! He turned pale, and his knees began to knock together. He summoned his royal advisors, but no one could explain what was happening, or what those words on the wall meant.

Finally, a fellow named Daniel was brought before the king to interpret this stunning event, and to translate the mysterious words on the wall. Daniel told the king that he had not humbled his heart, that he had defied the Lord, and that he had been glorifying the wrong gods. Furthermore, Daniel explained that the words on the wall prophesied that Belshazzar's kingdom would soon come to an end. Belshazzar met his doom that very night...not long after he saw the handwriting on the wall.

If you were to take a tour of a treatment center, you might have the opportunity to examine the group rooms, where the group therapy sessions take place. You probably would notice the large white boards, covered with writing. You might recognize the record of a person's drug and alcohol usage, delineated beneath headings like these: age/drug/amount/frequency/where/consequences.

Counselors routinely ask their patients to spell out the story of their drug and alcohol use on the walls, hoping this exercise will help the chemically dependent people to recognize what really has been going on in their lives, and where their abuse of chemicals is leading. Recovery begins with studying the handwriting on the wall, and perhaps in being properly horrified.

A sage once observed, "An alcoholic is a human being written large." I think this means that an alcoholic is a person with exaggerated defects of character; in zealous pursuit of happiness; with a desperate craving for love and acceptance and God.

An alcoholic is a HUMAN BEING (written large)! The process of recovery seems to have something to do with recognizing the handwriting on the wall.

How Do You Get the
Spiritual Part of the Program?

I once had a conversation with a man who asked me, "How do you get the spiritual side of the A.A. program?" He was undergoing treatment for his alcoholism after having had a relapse. He claimed that he had been to a lot of A.A. meetings, and that he knew all about the 12 Steps and the slogans, but that the spiritual dimension of his recovery was missing.

So, how do you get the spiritual part of the program? Before responding to this inquiry, the question itself warrants comment.

In the first place, it is futile to try to "figure out" the spiritual portion of the recovery process (if indeed this is what the man was trying to do). Spirituality simply does not yield to rational analysis. The things of the spirit are accessible only to those who are ready to stop intellectualizing and to start trusting instead. The Big Book captures this insight in what is known as "the metaphor of the electric light," the gist of which is that you do not have to understand how electricity works in order to turn on a light when you enter a room. You merely flip the switch.[39] The analogy is that spirituality is something simple; it eludes those who seek to master it through intellectual endeavor.

To come at the question from a different angle, one might observe that no one ever really *gets* the spiritual part of the A.A. program—at least not in the sense that it can be kept or stored or possessed. One does not actually *get* spirituality, although one might catch a glimpse of it. If you do *get* spirituality, you cannot hold it; you find it anew each day, or you do not find it at all. Spirituality is not about arriving at some sacred plateau, but the journey itself.

Furthermore, some say that there is no *spiritual side* to the A.A. program, anyway.[40] The whole program—every Step, every slogan, each tidbit of wisdom, each contact with peers— can be considered spiritual in its own right. Dr. Bob used to become annoyed when people would ask him about *the spiritual angle* of the program. "There is no spiritual angle," he would reply. "It's a spiritual program."[41] One who is seeking to identify the spiritual slice of the program might dwell upon this question first: Which part of the program is <u>not</u> spiritual?

A person who claims to be striving to *get the spiritual side of the program* needs to take care that he or she is not trying to *figure it out*, or to *capture it* in a fist, or to *reduce it* to something manageable. All of these approaches to spirituality manifest the need to control.

Now, having wrenched this man's question in a variety of ways, I shall respond to the question as he asked it of me in the first place. How do you get the spiritual side of the A.A. program?

The Big Book states flatly that "...no one need have difficulty with the spirituality of the program."[42] The key to achieving some sort of relationship with God or a Higher Power is identified in the acronym "H.O.W."[43] H.O.W. do you get the spiritual side of the program, but through <u>H</u>onesty, <u>O</u>penness, and <u>W</u>illingness? The man who was seeking the spiritual dimension of the recovery program might ask himself where he has not been completely honest, open, and willing.

Some say that there is no direct access to God, but that you can get a spiritual connectedness by committing yourself wholeheartedly to the program. Get yourself to a meeting; read the literature; work at the Steps; ask for help; and listen. Many people seem to find that their sense of spirituality comes "through the back door" when they apply themselves earnestly to the A.A. program.

How do you get the spiritual side of the A.A. program? If you are serious about wanting to establish a rapport with God, it would only make sense to begin with the practice of prayer or meditation. The most important thing to remember in this regard is that prayer is not about giving directions to God—or otherwise seeking to bend God's will to meet your own—but rather, learning to ask what God's will might be for you.

On one hand, Step 11 encourages prayer and meditation; on the other hand, it restricts the scope of prayer to asking what God wants me to do today, and for the courage to carry through with it. In other words, prayer in A.A. is not about insisting that "*My* will be done," but asking that "*Thy* will be done."

How do you get the spiritual part of the A.A. program? Here is another way to respond to the query:

> "I sought my soul, but my soul I could not see;
> I sought my God, but my God eluded me;
> I sought my brother, and found all three."[44]

Perhaps spirituality is found in human contact. Maybe we can discover the dimension called spiritual only as we enter into relationships with other people: in helping others; and learning to accept help from others; in finding compassion for others, and letting them care for us, too; or, in allowing trustworthy people to function as a "Higher Power" for us.

"How do you get the spiritual side of the program?" the man asked. Three potential answers to his question are: 1) through the *program* itself; 2) through *prayer*; or 3) through *people*.

In the end, I suppose the fellow was asking about how to have a "spiritual awakening." The Big Book makes it clear that a spiritual awakening does not have to be something dramatic or supernatural; it can also be something subtle and down-to-earth, like a change in attitude, an end to hatred, newfound compassion, or teachability.[45]

How do you achieve a spiritual awakening? The question seems to attract three other questions: Have you approached your recovery program with honesty, openness, and willingness? Have you asked God, or your Higher Power, for guidance? Have you given other people a chance to help you?

For one who is seeking the spiritual side of the recovery program, these might be some good places to start.

61

Gregory P. Gabriel

Here you go. You can photocopy this article and press it into the palm of your favorite preacher on your way out of church next Sunday. Or, you could pass it along to anyone who has ever wondered:

How to Hear a Fifth Step

Before addressing the question of "How to Hear a Fifth Step," it would make sense to establish "What is a Fifth Step?" and before this, "What is a Fourth Step?"

The Fourth Step of the A.A. program reads like this: "Made a searching and fearless moral inventory of ourselves." The Fourth Step involves making a list of your defects of character (your resentments or regrets, for example, and the times when you have been selfish or dishonest). Some people also include their positive personal qualities in their inventory of themselves.

The Fifth Step says "Admitted to God, to ourselves and to another human being the exact nature of our wrongs." When a person shares his or her inventory with a clergy (or whoever else might listen to this moral inventory), it constitutes a Fifth Step. Giving a Fifth Step is not exactly the same as going to confession, but it is closely related. The things that are said within the context of a Fifth Step, by the way, are considered completely confidential.

Having described the Fourth and Fifth Steps, we proceed to the matter of "How do you hear a Fifth Step?"

Let the emphasis rest not on the word *How*? but rather on the word *Hear*. When hearing a Fifth Step, there really is no technique to master, other than the simple art of listening. When you hear someone's Fifth Step, do not attempt to counsel or to *fix* that person's problems; rather, strive to listen carefully to the speaker. Spare the other person your deep pastoral insights, and your assorted words of wisdom. Do not moralize or *preach* at the person. Just listen.

There is nothing you can say in the context of a Fifth Step that will speak more meaningfully than your silence. A Fifth Step has a life of its own; your job is not to get in the way of the process. You may want to offer some feedback to the other person at the conclusion of the Fifth Step, but do not interrupt the Fifth Step itself unless it seems quite necessary. Be still.

Listening to a Fifth Step, very simply, means listening. Having made this point, there are a few minor things you might do to *guide* a Fifth Step, or to contribute to its integrity:

❑ Do not consent to hear the Fifth Step of someone who has not done a Fourth Step first. In other words, do not give your time and your attention to anyone who wants to "talk off the top of his or her head"—and still call it a Fifth Step. A person who brings no notes to a Fifth Step appointment, as a rule, is unprepared for the Step.

❑ Do not allow the Fifth Step presenter to digress, at least not to an extreme. If the person tends to ramble, or to stray into anecdotes unrelated to his or her own inventory, gently bring the presenter back to the purpose at hand. If the speaker wishes to discuss someone else's problems, remind the person to keep the focus on himself or herself.

❑ Do not let the Fifth Step presenter deal in generalities. Ask for specific examples. If a man admits, "I have been dishonest with my wife"—and clearly intends to let it go at this—you might ask him precisely how he has been dishonest. Generalizing, after all, is a form of defense.

There are times when it is appropriate to confront a person who is offering a Fifth Step (see the three examples above), but most of the Fifth Step ministry comes down to listening. Healing might come from God, or from within the person who gives a Fifth Step—but it does not come from you, the hearer of the Fifth Step. Your part is just to listen.

Hypocrisy and the Church

I once had a stirring conversation with a man who was undergoing treatment for his alcoholism. For the most part, he talked to me about the "hypocrisy" of the church. He complained about the sort of people who drink with both fists on Saturday night, cuss up a storm, and maybe even cheat on their spouses, and yet sit in the front row in church wearing their "Sunday-best" the next morning.

I think that he was implying that he himself had the decency not to show up at church after a night on the town—unlike the "phonies" and "holier-than-thou" sorts who frequent the churches. The man's appraisal of church folks was downright vicious. He made it clear that he wanted nothing to do with those hypocrites.

It is common to hear chemically dependent people voice their disdain for the church; frequently, the word hypocrisy is on their lips.

When I first started out as a parish pastor, and heard spiteful references to the phonies who go to church, I used to chirp, "Well, there is always room for one more!" Nowadays, however, I like to think there is a more mature response to this oh-so-common charge against the church.

I have heard the accusation of hypocrisy leveled against the church by chemically dependent people so zealously and so often that I shall pause to consider it—hopefully, without either defending the church unduly or castigating the institution unfairly. I consider myself both an agent of the church and a devotee of the 12 Steps and, as such, have a vested interest both in the integrity of the church and the viewpoint of the "recovering" community.

I suppose that there would be two ways to think of this charge of hypocrisy in the church: 1) There is <u>nothing</u> to the claim; or 2) There is <u>something</u> to the claim.

If a *hypocrite* is defined as "one who espouses certain values but does not live by them," it is apparent that such a definition would also fit the average alcoholic (whose life has become unmanageable due to the influence of alcohol). When an alcoholic complains about the lack of scruples among church folks, maybe...just maybe...it smacks of projection. The church, after all, is a convenient dumping ground for displaced anger.

Perhaps the reason why chemically dependent people so often rail against the phoniness of the church is that they themselves are poignantly unable to live within their own values. As the old saying goes: "The things I do not like about other people are the very things I cannot stand about myself."

I myself have been a church-goer all of my life (it is sort of expected of pastors) but I do not pick up the scent of hypocrisy in the church. Believe me, I do have my own pet complaints about the church, but hypocrisy is not one of them. My ecclesiastical frustrations simply have different names. If hypocrisy is characteristic of the church, I am not keenly aware of it.

One way to look at this issue is that this talk about phoniness in the church says more about the plaintiff than the accused. The other option, of course, is that the complaint is quite valid. Maybe there is a decided lack of integrity about the church as we know it. Perhaps it takes one who has struggled mightily to live within his or her own values (the alcoholic) to put a finger on this deficiency in the church.

I do not intend this as an insult against the church, but as a healthy exercise in self-examination: Do we of the church live by the values we profess? What sort of messages do we send to others by the way we lead our lives?

Is the church genuinely marred by hypocrisy? It is a question I shall leave in rhetorical form. Is there *nothing* to this charge? I am confident that you will form your own opinion on the subject, if you have not already.

In conclusion, I leave you with four thoughts that have occurred to me since my talk with the fellow who insisted that the church is a gathering of phonies. These four ideas emerge from the A.A. program itself, and might serve to govern any conversations among recovering people about hypocrisy in the church.

1) According to Tradition 10, "Alcoholics Anonymous has no opinion on outside issues," like the integrity of the church. You are entitled to your own personal views about the church, but A.A. has none.

2) The Big Book, citing Herbert Spencer, discourages "contempt prior to investigation."[46] Do you know for a fact that church folks consider themselves to be superior to others—or is this just what you infer?

3) It is one thing to have an opinion about the church; it is another thing to have a grudge. Bill W. put it this way: "We...beg you to lay aside prejudice, even against organized religion."[47]

4) A.A. is a selfish program. This is to say that I need not concern myself with the shortcomings of others (including church-goers); it is not my responsibility to take the inventory of others. It will be enough for me to strive to improve myself.

In the Days Before A.A.

Axel was a mean drunk.

He may have been a caring human being when he was not under the influence of alcohol, but liquor had a way of transforming this man into something evil. Whenever he drank, Axel became angry and argumentative—and even downright menacing.

Sometimes he threatened to shoot his own wife and young children if they did not do his bidding. At other times, he boasted that he would kill his brother's children. Such was the power that alcohol had over him.

Axel lost virtually everything he owned back in the early 1930's. Perhaps it was because of the Great Depression, or maybe it was the result of his own heavy drinking. In any case, there was a sheriff's auction in the front yard of his farm site in the fall of 1930. Almost everything was sold to pay the creditors. It must have been a humiliating experience for Axel and his family.

Axel's older brother lived on a farm across the road from Axel's place. His brother purchased Axel's decrepit automobile at the auction, apparently as a gesture of kindness. His brother allowed Axel to continue driving the old car, with the understanding that Axel would reimburse him as soon as he was able to do so. By the following February, however, Axel had not made any effort to pay off this debt, so his brother decided not to renew the car's license. He vowed to "junk" the old vehicle.

When his brother came to claim the automobile, Axel—who was intoxicated—flew into a rage. His brother, too, had been drinking, but he had the presence of mind to back away from Axel's fury. His brother managed to change the subject, which seemed to mollify Axel, at least for the moment. Things even calmed down enough for his brother to stay for supper with Axel and his family.

After the meal, however, the conversation returned to the matter of the car. Axel's anger was re-ignited. He lunged at his brother at the other side of the table with kicks and punches. A struggle ensued. His brother managed to pin Axel to the floor, but Axel still bellowed threats of murder. Fearing further violence, Axel's wife and four small children fled from the house.

When Axel finally got free, he bolted into the next room and reached for his shotgun. The two men fought for control of the weapon. Axel lost his footing, fell backwards, and struck his head on the stairstep.

Axel did not attempt to rise. He hardly stirred at all. His face turned pale, and he labored to breathe. His brother ran out the door to get help, but Axel expired before help could arrive. His death was ruled an accident.

I never did meet my grandfather. He died violently about 26 years before I was born. I have seen a grainy photograph of the man, but it is a distant shot, and his face is obscured by the shadow from the brim of his hat. He always has been a shadowy figure to me. I really know nothing of his life except for his last desperate struggle, which I have paraphrased from a single newspaper clipping. Those who knew him either have died themselves or are unwilling to talk about him.

The only thing I really know about my grandfather are the details of his final vicious struggle. I do not think that it would be fair to suggest that his tragic fight with his brother could represent his entire life, but it may well represent his wrenching struggle with alcoholism. Axel may have believed that he was fighting over a car, or a gun, or some matter of pride, but the real issue was his own demonic addiction to alcohol.

He lived and died before there was an A.A. program. In my mind, Axel personifies the anguish and struggle of a million alcoholics who lived before the help of A.A. was available. When I consider the details of his last hour, I am evermore convinced that no one actually wins a struggle with alcoholism. At best, we learn the wisdom of surrender.

69

Not a Very Spiritual Person

Some years ago I took four quarters of Clinical Pastoral Education (C.P.E.) at Hazelden (a chemical dependency treatment facility near Center City, Minnesota). Anyone who participates in this type of a chaplains' training program can expect to be evaluated frequently, and sometimes rigorously. Every three months I was appraised formally—and separately— by a chaplain supervisor, by colleagues on the job, and by fellow C.P.E. students.

Think of subjecting yourself to such regular scrutiny by others. In some ways, it was an emotional "boot camp." I got a lot of practice at receiving both affirmation and criticism from others—on my professional deportment as well as my own personal issues. Evaluation by others simply came with the territory.

(Just so that you know, the trick to receiving feedback graciously is to approach it from this angle: "I am okay as a person, but what might I learn about myself from others?")

In one evaluation session, I was taken to task by a counselor, who, shall we say, will never be mistaken for a modest person. The man made the observation that I did not seem, to him, to be "a very spiritual person." I remember his comment well!

At the time, I bristled at his remark. My blood began to boil, but one of the cardinal rules of the game is to *accept* whatever feedback is dumped into your lap. "Resist not!" goes the adage. I wanted in the worst way to fire back at him, "And do you consider *yourself* to be a spiritual person, Sir?" But I did not. I bit my tongue.

I did not answer the man that day, but I think I have been formulating a reply ever since then. Not a very spiritual person, you say?

I am told that if another person's words stir your ire you must, at some level, be in agreement with the person. Why else would you respond in anger unless, somehow, you concur with the opinion just expressed? In other words, if you believe that what the other person has said is truly ridiculous, why should it trouble you?

Now, I am not opposed to the suggestion that I am not a very spiritual person. In fact, I am convinced of this. It is just that *I* like to be the one who makes this assessment of myself. Frankly, I despise the thinking that pastors somehow seem to be "closer to God" than other folks. My favorite Beatitude has always been "Blessed are the poor in spirit." I just do not like it when other people put their finger on my spiritual poverty. I would rather do that myself.

Maybe I should be glad that I do not measure up to this man's lofty standards, by which a truly "spiritual person" is known. (No, wait. That sounds too resentful.)

I have been mulling over my defense for quite a while now. I think I have it underlined in a book called *Came to Believe*: "If God is a spiritual being, then we are spiritual beings."[48] I cannot say that I know exactly what this means, but it sounds like the kind of statement with which no one would dare to argue.

If you ever see that guy who charged that I was not a very spiritual person, tell him I said "hello." Let him know that I have been thinking of him. If he asks about me, tell him I am just about as spiritual as I used to be: spiritual enough to accept feedback from people (even those of his ilk) but not spiritual enough to forget about it.

On Our Knees

"Humbly asked Him to remove our shortcomings."
(Step Seven)

When Bill W. and Dr. Bob first started trying to help other alcoholics to stay sober, they required the alcoholics to get down *on their knees* in order to make their surrender to God.[49] I suspect that the practice of kneeling was a holdover from Bill's and Bob's background in the Oxford Group. In any case, the co-founders of A.A. seemed to believe that dropping to your knees was an essential part of turning your life over to God.

When Bill W. wrote the first draft of the 12 Steps of A.A., he clearly expected the adherents of the program to kneel. Step Seven originally read like this: "Humbly on our knees asked Him to remove our shortcomings."[50] Some of the early A.A. members objected to this pious posture, however, so the phrase "on our knees" was deleted from the Seventh Step. Today, the 12 Steps read essentially the way Bill W. first wrote them except for the mandate to get down on your knees.

I recall watching an animated movie called *Charlotte's Web* with my youngest son. It is a story about a spider named Charlotte who has the remarkable ability to spell out words in her web. As the plot develops, Charlotte wants to save her friend Wilbur, who is a pig, from being slaughtered, so she writes words in her webs that are intended to describe just how special her pal Wilbur really is.

One of the terms she plans to spin into her web is *humble*. When one of her barnyard buddies asks what this word means, Charlotte replies, "Humble has two meanings: It means 'not proud' and 'near the ground.'" The latter definition caught my attention. The term humble sounded like a Latin word, so I looked it up in a Latin-English dictionary. According to the dictionary, the word humble comes from the same root as the word *humus* (or *dirt*). Charlotte was right. To get humble literally does signify getting *near the ground.*

Now, I think it is ironic that some of the early A.A. members insisted that the phrase "on our knees" be excised from the Seventh Step. It is ironic because the idea of getting near to the dirt is still implied in the word *humbly* in Step Seven. Whether or not you literally fall on your knees, you still have to get close to the dirt in your life in order to work the 12 Steps. It is all wrapped up in the word *humbly* in Step Seven.

Humbleness is synonymous with *humility*—but not *humiliation*. Humiliation is something different; it suggests shame or injury. To be humble simply means to be human— nothing more, and nothing less. Some people seem to resist getting humble because they think it means humiliation, which it does not. Some patients in addictions treatment programs do not want their family members to participate in their treatment because they are afraid of being humiliated by a recitation of their misdeeds. Treatment is not about humiliating anyone, however; it is about getting humble.

Being humble means being able to listen to criticism without getting defensive. Becoming humble merely means to become teachable. It involves being a regular person, not an authority on all subjects or a "big shot." Psychiatrist Harry Tiebout wrote of *getting humble* in terms of "ego-deflation."[51] I myself like Charlotte the spider's definition the best, however: *humble* means *near to the ground*.

I remember a patient at an addictions treatment center who was a pompous, arrogant sort. He seemed to be quite proud of his professional station, even though he had not worked in years because of his alcoholism. He frequently made condescending remarks about people who were not "white-collar workers," as he viewed himself.

I came upon this same man a few months after his time in treatment. By this time he was living in a halfway house, and working at a job that involved manual labor. I think that he said that he had been repairing the bleachers at the county fairgrounds. I glanced at his soiled clothes. I noticed his dirty face and hands. He looked good. He was wearing a grin.

The grass stains on the knees of his pants verified that he had gotten near to the ground—which, after all, is what getting humble is all about.

Organized Religion

I once met a man at a treatment center who explained to me that he believed in God, but that he had "a bone to pick with organized religion." After our conversation, I thought about his choice of words, and wondered what he meant by the phrase *organized religion.*

It occurs to me that the phrase *organized religion* is not a neutral expression. It seems to have an unpleasant connotation...perhaps even an odor. *Organized religion* even sounds a bit like *organized crime.*

I am curious: Would the opposite of organized religion be *disorganized religion*?

As a pastor, I have known quite a few churches that were not, in any sense of the word, organized. I have experienced congregations that resisted organization; indeed, they were proud of their lack of organization. Why, I have seen churches that could not be organized with a whip and a chair...but I digress.

What is this entity called "organized religion"?

Does the expression *organized religion* suggest *institutional religion*? *Denominationalism*?

I think I do know why many churches are incorporated into larger denominations. There are some problems which simply cannot be addressed without some level of cooperation.

I defer to the man who once was head of my denomination, former ELCA Bishop H. George Anderson, who writes: "Our denominations were built around great causes—foreign missions, education, home missions, and the care of the aged and orphans—urgent needs that congregations could not address alone."[52]

Why do we need organized religion? We need some sort of organization in order to respond effectively to major social issues, like world hunger.

I suspect that this argument, however, would fail to impress the fellow who claimed to have a problem with organized religion. Allow me to try again.

Kathleen Norris is the author of a book called *Amazing Grace*, one chapter of which she devotes to the topic of *organized religion*. She notes, "I have come to suspect that when people complain about 'organized' religion, what they are really saying is that they can't stand other people."[53]

Norris could be right. Maybe people's problem with organized religion comes down to their essential problem with other people. If people are inclined to keep their religion to themselves, perhaps it is because they have felt hurt or disillusioned by their relationships with others. If people eschew the church, it may be because they have felt shamed or judged by others.

Perhaps the opposite of organized religion is not disorganized religion but private religion.

I do not have ready answers for those who complain about organized religion, but I shall share three thoughts which make sense to me: 1) Organized religion is not necessarily something vile; 2) In some ways, religion needs to be organized if it is to be effective; and 3) Many grievances against organized religion say more about trust that has been trampled (or the perception that trust has been trampled) than about organized religion itself.

Piles

I have a friend who is a pastor. This friend of mine has a problem with *clutter*—and he knows it.

He once told me about a time when he moved into town to begin a job as a parish pastor, of how he looked over his new office, and discovered that he had inherited a mound of paper, three-feet high. His predecessor had left town a few months before, and the church's mail had accumulated in a corner during the interim. The bills had been extracted from this enormous heap, but the rest remained: the correspondence, the catalogues, the magazines, the newsletters, the advertisements, and the et cetera.

The pastor began to sift through this formidable pile, but the task proved to be more difficult than he had anticipated. In fact, the chore was overwhelming. Although he disposed of many of the papers, and took action on some others, he still found that there was a great quantity which he could not quite throw away, or file, or deal with otherwise. He could not bring himself to dispose of some of it because he thought he might be able to use it someday. He could not file it, either, because he was not able to figure out a category for it. Disgustedly, he pitched some of the papers back onto the stack.

As the months went by, this paper monster continued to grow, despite his repeated attempts to combat it. New items arrived in the mail every day, some of which found their way onto this onerous heap. Eventually, the stack became two. Then the pastor found himself stepping over several piles in his office. Instead of slaying the dragon in the corner, he realized, he was feeding it.

I myself have been thinking about clutter lately. Maybe it is a spiritual matter. I have a theory that a person's piles are tangible evidence of some unresolved personal issues.

I suspect that piles have something to do with guilt. A stack of unfinished business in the corner is an excellent excuse to feel guilty. Maybe our piles represent guilt. What is a pile, but a collection of unmade decisions? A *decision* problem often comes down to being a *guilt* problem.

The *Courage to Change* book suggests that our clutter isolates us.[54] Perhaps those paper towers really amount to *walls* that are intended to keep other people away.

Or are piles about fear? Maybe people find security, or comfort, in their messes—like a sow in the mud. Perhaps we come to rely on our piles to keep us safe. Maybe we place our trust in our stacks of stuff. Piles signify the fear of letting go, perhaps of our old selves.

Surely, our piles speak of our priorities, or rather, the inability to establish priorities (knowing what to save, and what to toss). When the thought that "I-might-need-that" runs amuck, we keep everything, and priorities vanish.

When we speak of genuine guilt, of utter aloneness, of deepest security, and ultimate priorities, we speak of spirituality.

I am reminded of a speaker who rehearsed what he called the "Six Universals of A.A." In essence, he outlined how to work the A.A. program:

1) Get honest.
2) Get with people who are getting honest.
3) Find a Higher Power.
4) Clean house.
5) Get in shape.
6) Pass it on.

I am especially interested in the fourth item on this list: *Clean house.* The speaker explained that this phrase is meant metaphorically—something like "Examine your moral principles"—but I like to dwell on the literal interpretation. Clean house. You want some spirituality? So start by making your bed. You say you are in search of serenity? First lose the pile in the back room. If you are interested in putting your house in order, you can start by putting your house in order.

There is something cleansing about cleaning. There is something energizing about picking up a pile and dealing with it. *Letting go* is an essential human task. In prosaic terms, it is important to *clean house*.

I once heard a counselor observe that people who are ready to make an important change in their life often start by cleaning up their messes. In and of itself, tidying up the house might not be deeply significant, but then again, it could represent an act of preparation for something else.

I have a theory that dealing successfully with piles comes down to two things:1) making decisions more aggressively about what to save and what to relinquish; and 2) learning what it means to *let go*.

I have reason to believe that my pastor-friend will be "cleaning house" in his office very soon. Maybe this weekend.

Religion Revisited

Back when I was in college, I "blew out" my right knee while playing intramural basketball. I was driving in for a lay-up when someone shoved me hard from behind, just as I was planting my right foot. I felt something snap in my knee. I yelped and crumpled to the floor. The pain subsided quickly, but the swelling in my knee persisted for weeks.

Unable to bend my knee, I spent the next month on crutches. On the Sunday after the mishap, I went to the front of the church to receive Holy Communion and then realized that I was not able to kneel. "Well, God," I mused, "if you want me to pray, you are going to have to heal my knee."

A physician informed me that I had torn the anterior cruciate ligament in my knee. He also cautioned me that reconstructive surgery was something drastic and that rehabilitation could take six months. I still remember his words of advice: "Unless you plan to play NBA basketball, I suggest that you live with it." And I *have* lived with the damaged ligament.

In a way, I suppose that this wound represented an end-of-innocence for me. Young people do tend to operate with the assumption that they are indestructible, at least until some crucial experience brings them down—in my case, to the gymnasium floor.

Did you know that the word "**lig**ament" comes from the same Latin root as the word "re**lig**ion"?

If a *ligament* is the tissue that holds your bones and cartilage together, than I suppose that *religion* is whatever holds your life or worldview together. Many people seem to disparage the word *religion*, including some in the A.A. community. However, I think it is a richer concept than many people suspect.

The word *religion* rarely occurs in the Bible (in its English translation). The term religion does not appear at all in the Old Testament. Gerhard von Rad, a famous biblical scholar, maintains that the closest thing to the notion of religion in the

80

Old Testament might be the concept of obedience.[55] Obedience to the will of God—perhaps this is the essence of religion.

I once heard a man declare, with conviction, "I am not a religious person." I wondered what he meant—that he did not go to church, or did not read the Bible? I would like to think that the word religion means something more than this.

I remember reading a memoir written by a woman named Patricia Hampl. The author had grown up in the Catholic Church and had attended Catholic schools but, as an adult, had distanced herself from the Catholic Church. (Incidentally, many people who come to treatment for their addictions also seem to feel estranged from their churchly upbringings.) Hampl came to the conclusion, however, that something was missing from her life. "It was the instinct to bow the head," she writes, "to bend the knee."[56]

Is this not what religion really is about? The impulse to kneel? Bowing, yielding to a will greater than your own? Accepting torn ligaments and other things you cannot change?

Sooner or later, everyone's sense of religion suffers a blow, and it usually is more devastating than the trauma to my knee. Then people face the task of examining their religion, and asking what it is that will hold their life and their world together.

Remembering William James

When Bill W. wrote the Big Book of A.A. back in 1938, he cited only one book and only one author.[57] That would be *The Varieties of Religious Experience* by William James. Bill W. acknowledged that he was deeply influenced by the writings of William James. In fact, Bill W. once spoke of William James as a "founder of Alcoholics Anonymous."[58]

William James was a philosopher and a psychologist who taught at Harvard from 1873 until 1907. He and Ralph Waldo Emerson commonly are regarded as the most eminent philosophers in American history.

William James was born in New York City in 1842. His father was a renowned theologian by the name of Henry James, and his brother was a famous novelist by the same name. James received something of an elitist education in private schools in New York and in various cities in Europe. At one time he aspired to be a painter, but he turned his attention to chemistry and anatomy when he enrolled at Harvard in 1861. Three years later, James entered Harvard Medical School. Although he was awarded the M.D. degree in 1869, he decided that he had little interest in practicing medicine.

James struggled with a variety of health problems throughout his life. He floundered vocationally as well, until he secured a teaching position at Harvard. James began lecturing in the areas of physiology and anatomy, but soon made a transition to philosophy and psychology, even though the only degree he himself ever attained was M.D. William James was a man with an exceedingly broad background in science, literature, and the arts.

William James emphasized some philosophical concepts called "pragmatism" and "pluralism." He maintained an active interest in the relationship between mind and body, between psychology and physiology. He is credited with founding the first psychological laboratory in The United States.

Professor James gained fame after he published a book entitled *The Principles of Psychology* in 1890. He traveled to Edinburgh, Scotland to deliver the prestigious Gifford lecture series in 1901-02. The substance of these lectures was incorporated into the book called *The Varieties of Religious Experience*, which later would make a profound impression upon Bill W.

In some ways, William James and Bill W. were kindred spirits. Both were eccentric types, imbued with "pioneering personalities." Each man experienced deep depressions and nervous breakdowns. Both William James and Bill W. took an interest in psychic phenomena (clairvoyance, communicating with the "spirit world," and the like). Neither William James nor Bill W. ever found a home in institutional religion, but both were earnestly committed to the pursuit of spiritual questions.

What exactly did Bill W. find in the writings of William James that so intrigued him? I think that Bill W. was especially enthusiastic about the things the great philosopher wrote about *conversion.*

Bill W. read *The Varieties of Religious Experience* at a time when he was struggling to get a grip on his own sobriety. He disliked the term *conversion* (because of the connotations some strident religious people had attached to it) but he did seem to need to hear that some sort of fundamental inner change was indeed possible, and that it was something real. He needed to hear it from a highly respected philosopher, too.

The Varieties of Religious Experience is a book teeming with human case studies, many of which suggest that different types of people can have different ways of experiencing divine influence. Perhaps this book gave Bill W. some sense of permission to trust his own instincts and perceptions about *spiritual awakenings* (an expression Bill W. preferred to *conversion*). No doubt, he was gratified to read that a spiritual awakening can dawn on people in a great many different ways.

When Bill W. read that a *conversion experience* need not be something sudden and spectacular, but rather that it might be

83

something subtle or gradual, his own suspicions were confirmed. He warmed to the idea of a spiritual awakening of an "educational variety."[59]

Bill W. paid tribute to the renowned philosopher with these words: "Thus, William James firmed up the foundation on which I and many others have stood all these years."[60]

Revelation

As a chaplain at an addictions treatment center, I have heard a lot of alcoholics talk about God. Most of them (but not all) seem to want to refer to their Higher Power as "God."

Some of them endeavor to describe the essence of God ("He's a spirit"), or the appearance of God ("He's like an old man with a long, white beard who wears a robe and sits on a throne with a staff in his hand"). One of the more thoughtful patients I have encountered came to a different conclusion, however: "I really don't know what God is like. I just know that I am doing the things my counselor asks me to do, and that something is working for me."

The last observation strikes me as something more profound than the former comments. There is something to be said for knowing what you do not know about divine things. As a matter of fact, I think that A.A. places an emphasis upon not naming God. A few cases-in-point from "recovery" literature would seem to be in order:

❑   "I have no idea Who or What is running the show, but I know I'm not!"[61]

❑   "I don't need to understand the Power greater than myself, only to trust it."[62]

❑   "You can't define this Higher Power."[63]

❑   "If you can name it, it's not God." (Father Dowling, a spiritual advisor to Bill W.[64])

There is a certain wisdom about declining to be specific about divine matters. A.A. has a way of reveling in the mystery of God.

85

I admired the absence of pious precision in the philosophy of
A.A.—at least until I came upon a man who had been a friend of
mine and a fellow student during my days at the seminary. He
explained to me that he had returned to the seminary to pursue a
doctoral degree in systematic theology (which would be
something about organizing and interpreting religious thinking).
He told me about his work and his family, and I told him about
mine.

When I described my work at an addictions treatment center,
he nodded his approval. "A.A. is a good program," he observed.
"It has helped millions of people. The only problem with A.A.,"
he added, "is that there is no revelation."

"Some people find no revelation *in the church*," I replied,
only slightly in jest.

He glared at me for a long moment, but said nothing. After
an uneasy pause, we changed the subject.

In retrospect, I should have known better than to cross
swords with a systematic theologian. He could have diced me up
then and there. Maybe he spared me because he still regarded me
as a friend.

I still remember his remark, though: There is no revelation in
A.A. I think I know what he meant by this, too. In the Christian
tradition, God makes himself known in a tangible form: the
Christ-child who is born in Bethlehem. In A.A. thinking,
however, the presence of God is something more speculative,
something more abstract than a gurgling baby.

In A.A., spirituality is often discussed in terms of looking for
coincidences, of keeping an open mind, of trusting, or of
wondering what God's will might be. Is something essential
missing from the philosophy of A.A.? Something concrete? Does
A.A. lack revelation?

Well, I am not sure.

This much I do know: The word *revelation* means something
different to a systematic theologian than it does to the average
A.A. member. A Christian systematic theologian might assert
that God makes himself known through a sacred story, but in

A.A., what is held sacred is a person's own individual story. While the church lays claim to a certain kind of revelation, A.A. possesses its own brand of revelation. There is revelation *from on high* and there is revelation that comes *from within*.

The church has a meaningful story to tell, especially at Christmas time. In A.A., however, telling your own story becomes your own salvation history.

Gregory P. Gabriel

Rigorous Reading

Al-Anon publishes a bookmark that is entitled *Just for Today*. Printed on this bookmark are nine different suggestions about how to live out the 12-Step program. One of the suggestions is this:

"Just for today I will try to strengthen my mind. I will study. I will learn something useful. I will not be a mental loafer. I will read something that requires effort, thought and concentration."[65]

Al-Anon's advice, in other words, is to tackle something more substantial than the popular magazines or the romance novels near the check-out counter at the grocery store. It is easy to get into the habit of reading "fluffy stuff," but Al-Anon advocates trying some literature that is more challenging.

I myself took an English major back in college, which involved a good deal of reading. Nonetheless, I find that the further I get from my years of formal education, the more difficult it becomes to read anything of substance. Yes, I do take time to read, but I do not seem to read things that are of the same caliber as the materials I pored over during my years in academia.

My point is that Al-Anon encourages folks to read something challenging once in a while. It is true that the 12-Step program has a marked preference for simplicity, and an aversion to intellectualizing, and a general emphasis upon "being gentle with yourself in recovery"—all of which would commend light reading. Still, there comes a time when it might be helpful to indulge in some reading that is rigorous.

I once heard a speaker warn about what he termed "the dumbing of America." He pointed out that the vast body of recovery literature now on the market is geared to a junior high reading level. On one hand, these materials are accessible to a

88

wide range of readers, but on the other hand, he admonished, it also serves to dull the collective American intelligence. He charged that self-help books contribute to the "dumbing of America."

Now, I do not know about you, but I would not want to be accused of being "dumb" or, as the Al-Anon bookmark puts it, a "mental loafer." Thus, I bravely plucked a formidable-looking book from my shelf and cracked it open: *The Varieties of Religious Experience* by William James. It is a scholarly monograph, written a century ago by a philosopher from Harvard. I chose this particular book, first of all, because it was treasured by Bill W. and Dr. Bob, and secondly, because it looked, uh, hard.

Although it took me a fortnight, I slogged through this entire book, all 397 pages of it. I came upon some interesting thoughts in the book, but for the most part, the book impressed me as something stuffy and esoteric—which is why I read it in the first place.

I do not intend to comment any further on this book, but I would like to lift up a single quote from William James on the subject of drinking. The book is not at all focused on the use of alcohol, but the author does make this passing remark on the subject: "To the poor and the unlettered it stands in the place of symphony concerts and of literature..."[66] I think that Professor James suggests that people who are not acquainted with the arts and with books tend to occupy themselves with drinking.

If this observation strikes you as a bit condescending (as it does me), please bear in mind that he wrote these words about a hundred years ago, long before there was A.A., or much talk about alcoholism-as-disease. I do not think that William James had a thorough understanding of alcoholism-as-a-disease, but in his own erudite way, he makes an interesting comment about a place in people's lives that may come to be occupied either by alcohol or by books.

Someone once observed that a good book creates space in a person's life. Maybe a good book can prepare the way for prayer or spiritual insight. Sometimes a good book is light reading; at other times, Al-Anon notes, it is something weighty.

Silence

"Be still, and know that I am God."
(Psalm 46)

They sat in a circle of silence. The only sound was the boiling of the coffee in the pot. No one had volunteered to lead the Al-Anon meeting, as often was the case, so they all sat quietly. One woman asked if anyone had anything that he or she needed to talk about, but no one spoke. No one even stirred. Only the coffee-maker struggled against the tranquility.

There was nothing boring or anxious about that moment of quiet. People appeared to be alert, and "tuned in," as well. They just did not have anything to say. There was something comfortable, something satisfying about the silence. I think that a lot of people go to Al-Anon meetings for just such a moment of calm.

This particular meeting started slowly, but silence is an integral part of every Al-Anon meeting. It is a custom to begin an Al-Anon meeting with a moment of silence followed by The Serenity Prayer. That pause before the prayer might be more important than any other part of the meeting which follows. It is a time to collect yourself, a time to establish yourself in the present. There is a spiritual quality about stillness. Some say that the language of God is silence.

I remember the tale of an A.A. veteran who recalled the very first meeting he ever attended. When he arrived at the door, an older man sized him up, and then asked him gruffly, "This your first meetin'?"

"Yep," replied the first man, nervously.

"Well, then," said the man by the door, "get yourself a cup of coffee and sit down and shut up—because you don't know nuthin' anyway."

This is an inexcusably rude way to greet a newcomer to A.A., and yet, there is also something appropriate about this sort of a welcome. The invitation to have a cup of coffee is about hospitality, and the observation that "you don't know nuthin' anyway" is about getting humble. In between is the admonition to "Sit down and shut up," which is nothing more than an extremely crude way to say, "Be still, and know that I am God."

One could make the case that the whole process of recovery begins with silence. A person simply does not make progress in A.A. or Al-Anon until he or she has learned to be quiet. It is a spiritual program; it all starts with stillness. If you desire to develop conscious contact with God, prayer begins with silence. If you struggle in your relationships with others, you might quit arguing. Keep still. If you have a tendency to berate yourself, you could strive to catch yourself in the act and just be quiet instead. Listen to the crackle of the coffee pot.

In A.A. and Al-Anon, everything seems to come back to silence. To be blunt, the key is to "Sit down and shut up." In more gracious terms, the key is to "Be still, and know that I am God."

On one hand, silence is an essential aspect of recovery; on the other hand, however, it can be an obstacle to recovery. Ironically, it is silence that sometimes keeps people "sick," or at least testifies to their problems.

Sometimes people express their anger by becoming quiet. In such a case, silence might be intended to punish. In other instances, entire families live by a "no-talk" rule, an unspoken agreement founded upon fear. In either situation, recovery is not about preserving the silence, but breaking it.

I once heard a woman complain that her alcoholic husband simply would not speak. She claimed that he would lie on the couch, facing the wall, and would not utter a word—not a word!—sometimes for a full week. The man would come to the table for meals with his family, but he would not respond to questions and he would not account for himself in any way. His complete silence said a great deal about how he was feeling about himself. In deepest shame, people cannot quite find words. It requires a certain level of emotional health to be able to speak up, to dispel the silence.

For some folks, recovery is about learning to keep still. For others, it is about finding their voices.

> "For everything there is a season...a time to
> keep silence, and a time to speak."
> (Ecclesiastes 3)

Some Provocative Thoughts
About Prayer and Meditation

Here is a discussion-starter for your next A.A. or Al-Anon meeting: some provocative thoughts about prayer and meditation from the literature of the 12 Steps.

1) "So I began to pray: to place my problems in God's hands."
   (*Alcoholics Anonymous*, page 237)

2) "Many people pray as though to overcome the will of the reluctant God, instead of taking hold of the willingness of a loving God."
   (*Came to Believe*, page 26)

3) "The important part is not to cancel our prayers by later worrying."
   (*Came to Believe*, page 26)

4) "This is prayer: not to ask for anything but guidance."
   (*One Day at a Time in Al-Anon*, page 22)

5) "All true prayer somehow confesses our absolute dependence on God."
   (*One Day at a Time in Al-Anon*, page 22)

6) "Prayer is simply a reaching out to make contact with a Power greater than ourselves."
   (*One Day at a Time in Al-Anon*, page 123)

7) "Prayer, then, is not the act of giving directions to God, but to ask to learn his will."
   (*One Day at a Time in Al-Anon*, page 156)

8) "Am I too busy to pray? Have I no time for meditation? Then let me ask myself whether I have been able to solve my problems without help."
(*One Day at a Time in Al-Anon*, page 177)

9) "If I could get what I pray for, would it really make me happy?"
(*One Day at a Time in Al-Anon*, page 275)

10) "Asking Him to remove my faults is prayer at its best."
(*Al-Anon Family Groups*, page 46)

11) "My whole life is God speaking to me."
(*As We Understood...*, page 90)

12) "I have gone through various methods of praying and have now settled for just thanking God for my blessings."
(*As We Understood...*, page 204)

13) "Meditation is not what you think."
(*As We Understood...*, page 217)

14) "I think I have developed an understanding of God that I don't fully understand."
(*As We Understood...*, page 226)

15) "Almost the only scoffers at prayer are those who never tried enough."
(*Twelve Steps and Twelve Traditions*, page 97)

16) "We discover that we do receive guidance for our lives to just about the extent that we stop making demands upon God to give it to us on order and on our terms."
(*Twelve Steps and Twelve Traditions*, page 104)

Gregory P. Gabriel

17) "If you worry, why pray? If you pray, why worry?"
    (*Alcoholism: The Family Disease*, page 33)

18) "With prayer I say I am willing to be helped."
    (*Courage to Change*, page 182)

96

Spiritual Awakenings
and the Animal Kingdom

Many recovering alcoholics identify their *spiritual awakening* with some manifestation of the animal kingdom. Stories abound of people whose eyes were opened, in dramatic fashion, by an encounter with a wild animal or pet.

I remember the man who claimed that he awoke from a drunken sleep on a sidewalk—and found himself eye-to-eye with a gray squirrel. Even in his groggy condition, the man was astounded that the squirrel did not scurry away as squirrels always do. The squirrel stood stalk-still, gazing into his eyes from a distance of three feet. This encounter made a deep impression upon the man: for once in his life, someone (or something) did not flee from him.

Then there was the fellow who had received some heavy confrontation from his therapy group at an addictions treatment center. He was feeling "stung" and went outside to sit on a bench by himself to "lick his wounds." He happened to catch sight of a Monarch butterfly, and for some reason, opened his palm to the creature. To his astonishment, the butterfly lit upon his hand. He was deeply touched. Amazing things can happen, it occurred to him, when a person reaches out with an open hand.

There is also the tale of the woman who did not realize how much she had isolated herself until the day she sold her parrot at a pawnshop. It dawned on her then, with full force, that she had disposed of her only friend. She realized that she had already driven away everyone else who had ever cared about her. When the woman thought about what she had done to her parrot, she saw herself with a painful clarity. This moment marked the beginning of her recovery from chemical dependency.

In their hour of greatest need, people sometimes are able to bond with an animal in a way they cannot with other human beings. At some primal depth, people discover a kinship with birds or beasts that they are unable to find with their own kind. (At the risk of verging on the subject of religion, it seems that the Christmas story, about Jesus being born in a stable, bears out this theme: sometimes acceptance is to be found only among the animals.)

Of all the fauna that are credited with stirring something *spiritual* within the human breast, there is something unique about dogs. Above all of the others, the dog is a spiritual creature. The canine is known for its loyalty. No matter how rough your day has been, a dog is a devoted friend. A dog is a spiritual creature. (You know what you get when you spell *dog* backwards, don't you? Think about it.)

Having established that there is something uniquely spiritual about dogs, I confess that I do not like dogs. (It probably has something to do with the German Shepherd that punctured my palm when I was five. I thought he merely wanted to lick.)

The truth is that we do not have any pets at all at our house, although I am reminded of a time when our sons, respectively, were about 18-months-old. There was a point in their lives when they were slightly more like creatures than Homo sapiens.

In retrospect, I do not know that I could compare them to any particular animal, but they would greet me eagerly each day when I came home from work, and if they had tails, they would have been wagging excitedly. They whimpered sometimes, tugged at my shoelaces, and even "messed" the carpet, on occasion, if I was not swift enough with the diaper change. They climbed all over me, and even drooled on me, when I laid on the living room carpet.

Yes, I remember living in puppydom. I liked it a lot! If a spiritual awakening is when something opens your eyes to that which is ultimately important in life, then I have had such an experience. While I cannot claim to have had one grand spiritual awakening, I have had a great many puppy-sized ones.

Come to think of it, I have been missing a slipper for some time now.

Spirituality Versus Religion

"We hear it over and over again, in both AA and Al-Anon: this program is spiritual, not religious."[67]

Sometimes I get irritated when I hear people talking about the difference between spirituality and religion.

Recently, I heard a woman assert, "Religion is about promoting doctrine, but spirituality is about how human beings experience their Higher Power." As I considered her words, I went into a slow burn. Have you ever noticed that whenever spirituality is compared to religion, that the latter comes off as the sick sister?

I remember a day when I made a 140-mile trip (one-way) to a hospital to call on an older man who had undergone hip surgery. I chatted with this fellow for about half-an-hour, said a prayer with him, and then left for home.

I did not know the man very well, but he was a member of my congregation, and I was the pastor of his church. I called on him as a representative of the church (of religion!). I hoped that my visit would convey the message that the congregation remembered him in that faraway hospital, and that God remembered him, too. I called on him as an agent of the church, but—I cannot state this with enough emphasis—I did not go to see him to "promote doctrine."

When people differentiate between spirituality and religion, it often seems that the concept of religion is subject to caricature. It is cheapened. The idea of religion becomes the foil by which we understand spirituality.

Hoo, boy! Don't get me started! Don't get me started!

Someone once mused that religion can be likened to a peanut butter and jelly sandwich, but spirituality is just the bread alone. In other words, religion involves all kinds of extra glop (mostly empty calories) while spirituality is that which is truly essential. Once again, the distinction between spirituality and religion celebrates the former at the expense of the latter—and it gets my dander up, too!

I came upon a wizened old cowboy at an A.A. meeting who spelled out the difference between spirituality and religion with a raspy voice and an air of authority: "Religion is for people who are afraid of going to hell, but spirituality is for those who have already been there."

Give me a break.

I sincerely hope that Christian piety is not centered around the fear of eternal damnation. Let us not reduce religion to the desire to avoid hellfire. I have little doubt that this old cowpoke had known more than his share of suffering in his lifetime, but there are other people who have suffered, too—and some who have found meaning in their religion in the here-and-now.

A.A. understands itself as a spiritual program, although not a religious program. What exactly is the difference?

There probably is less that distinguishes spirituality from religion than some people suppose. Frankly, it is very difficult to define either word satisfactorily. Most of the characteristics of spirituality can also describe religion, and vice versa. Maybe there is no essential difference between spirituality and religion. I suspect that the distinction between spirituality and religion is mostly an illusion...albeit a helpful illusion. It is an important illusion.

If there is a substantive difference between spirituality and religion, it might have something to do with the word *should*. There is no *should* in A.A. Sometimes the word *should* crops up in the church—sometimes—but spirituality is a realm where there is no *should*.

Often, it does seem to help people in treatment when they distinguish spirituality from religion. It frees them to think of God or a Higher Power in any way that makes sense to them. It liberates them from old, and sometimes oppressive, ways of thinking about faith. When people speak in terms of spirituality, they give themselves permission to affirm their own values and consciences and personal beliefs. The notion of spirituality is not so much the antithesis of religion as it is the opposite of the word *should*.

I have great respect for the concept of spirituality. I am in favor of distinguishing spirituality from religion, if this distinction is helpful. I do not think that we need to denigrate religion, however, in order to appreciate spirituality. I do not think that *religion* is such a dirty word after all.

There. Got that off my chest.

Suicide

"We gambled to the point where it resulted in imprisonment, insanity or even attempted suicide."[68]

As a chaplain at an addictions treatment center, one of my duties is to facilitate a weekly grief group. Many people who come to treatment for chemical dependency or compulsive gambling are troubled by the death of a loved one, so we spend some time talking about significant losses, as well as addictions.

Some people in treatment are struggling with the suicide of a family member or friend. It is hard enough to cope with the sudden death of someone who is important to you, but it can be even more difficult to deal with the fact that someone took his or her own life. Some people contend with their sense of loss after a suicide with increased gambling or drinking.

Many people who have experienced the suicide of a loved one seem to have the idea that their family member or friend cannot possibly be admitted into heaven after having ended his or her own life. Quite a number of patients have told me, with a mixture of anguish and conviction, that it says in the Bible that no one who takes his own life can ever hope to go to heaven. Thus, their grief is compounded not only by the issue of suicide, but also by the fear of eternal judgment.

Sometimes I point out to people that any compulsive gambler who continues to place bets is already practicing a form of slow suicide, and that any alcoholic who persists in drinking is already pounding nails in his or her own coffin.

Sometimes I confront the notion that anyone who commits suicide is barred from heaven. Various churches have their own teachings about the eternal consequences of suicide, of course, but the Bible itself is silent on this subject.

Pardon me if I become a bit pedagogical here, but the Bible does not condemn those who have taken their own life. The word *suicide* does not even occur in the Bible (in its English translation). As a matter of fact, there are only a few examples in the Scriptures of people ending their own lives (Saul and his armor-bearer in 1 Samuel 31:4-5; Ahithophel in 2 Samuel 17:23; Zimri in 1 Kings 16:18; and Judas Iscariot in Matthew 27:5). Contrary to popular belief, the Bible does not explicitly forbid suicide, nor does it denounce those who have taken their own life.

Yes, there is a commandment which states, "Thou Shall Not Kill," but the Hebrew verb (*rah-tsahkh*) that is translated as "kill" usually pertains to the murder of a neighbor, not self-destruction.

I do believe that God is in favor of life, and that God is opposed to self-destruction. When someone commits suicide, however, I prefer to think that God is moved to grief, not wrath.

I tend to think that no one really wants to die. When people commit suicide, it is because they cannot stand the pain that is a part of their life, a pain that sometimes is caused by their addiction. If you believe in the charity and compassion of God ("the *care* of a Power greater than ourselves," as Step Three states), it would be conceivable that God could understand the human pain that could push some people to the brink of self-destruction. Letting go of the idea that God punishes those who have ended their own life is one part of the task of letting go of a conception of a God who is angry and vindictive.

No, I do not believe that God condemns those who have taken their own life.

Taking a Tunk

There is a quaint old expression in New England: "taking a tunk."[69] It means going for a walk.

Bill W. was a native of Vermont, and therefore, was acquainted with this old-fashioned phrase. In the days before the A.A. program had been established—in the days before Bill W.'s own sobriety was secure—he traveled to Akron, Ohio on a business trip. Wilson found himself alone in the lobby of the Mayflower Hotel, wishing he had a drink, and yet, feeling terrified of the consequences of ordering one.

Bill W. was desperate. He scanned a directory of the churches and ministers in Akron and chose the Rev. Walter F. Tunks—perhaps because the minister's surname reminded him of the old Vermont expression ("taking a tunk"). Bill W. called Rev. Tunks and asked for the name of another alcoholic. Rev. Tunks referred him to one Norman Sheppard, who put him in touch with Henrietta Seiberling, who ultimately introduced him to Dr. Robert Smith—another native of Vermont and a struggling alcoholic with whom Bill W. would organize the A.A. movement.

I like to think that the genesis of A.A. is somehow associated with the notion of taking a walk. It may well have been the word "tunk" that set in motion the chain of events that brought together Bill Wilson and Dr. Bob Smith. Perhaps it was the key word "tunk" that brought all of the tumblers of heaven into place so that the A.A. program could be established.

If the origin of A.A. is related to the thought of going for a walk, it would seem appropriate. There is something intrinsically spiritual about walking—simply walking. It is an unhurried gait. Unless you are into "power-walking," it is a tangible way to slow yourself down.

Sometimes, the patients at addictions treatment centers are required to do some walking. Officially, this activity might be called *exercise*, but it could just as well be termed *therapy*.

Walking is good medicine for whatever ails you. The simple motion of walking can offer a different perspective on life's problems.

One patient told me that he realized he was beginning to make progress in his treatment program when he started to notice things on his morning walks: a rabbit crouched in the bushes, or the buds on the trees. Walking does seem to be related to *noticing*, and *noticing* akin to spirituality.

Bill W. and his wife Lois were inveterate hikers. It was something they did together throughout their married life. In her memoirs, Lois recalls their habit of walking: "When we were tired or unable to solve some problem, we would go off by ourselves in the woods or occasionally by the sea. It did not always solve the problem, but we were better able to think clearly after such a renewal of body and soul."[70]

Maybe it does not matter what you do about your life's problems, as long as you do it for the right reasons. You could build a snowman, or you could roll down a grassy hill, or you could take a tunk—any of which might be deeply therapeutic for a troubled soul—as long as it is done in the name of self-care.

The *One Day at a Time in Al-Anon* book tells the tale of a person who came to an Al-Anon meeting, and shared some of the woe of living with an alcoholic. The person pleaded to know, "What shall I do?"

Then came the reply: "Do the dishes! Take a walk! Read a book! Start somewhere to unhook your mind from confusions, but don't do anything about your problems until you can see them more clearly."[71]

Someone once observed that "Walking is simply the process of falling forward, then catching yourself just before you land flat on your face." Maybe recovery is supposed to be just this simple, too. Maybe the whole recovery process can begin with "taking a tunk."

Gregory P. Gabriel

Tales from Papua New Guinea

Papua New Guinea is located on an island, just north of Australia. The country is covered with mountains and thick rain forests. The indigenous people are dark-skinned people, called Melanesians. While some of the inhabitants of Papua New Guinea live, literally, in the Stone Age, others lead relatively modern lives in the larger cities.

Over the years, white people have been coming to Papua New Guinea from Australia, Europe, and the United States, in order to explore, establish mines and plantations, and propagate the Christian faith. I myself traveled to Papua New Guinea some years ago, along with a contingent of other Lutherans from the United States, in order to examine the fruits of the mission work in that country. During my sojourn in Papua New Guinea, I did get to see how the church has taken root in another culture—but I also found out that alcohol problems have taken root, as well.

Alcohol was illegal in Papua New Guinea until 1962, we were told. Before this time, the white business people and missionaries brought their own alcoholic beverages into the country in defiance of the law, but the Melanesian people were forbidden to buy or sell or consume the stuff. Understandably, the situation created tension. The natives of Papua New Guinea asked why they could not have alcohol if the white foreigners could.

On one hand, the government did not want to legalize alcohol for everyone, for fear of the problems which might ensue. On the other hand, the government could not enforce the ban on alcohol without stirring the wrath of the white people who lived and worked in the country. They say that some of the German missionaries threatened to go back to Deutschland if they could not have their beer.

Finally, in 1962, the government did legalize alcohol in Papua New Guinea. As one problem was solved, however, other issues arose. It seems that the natives of Papua New Guinea had no money—literally, no money—with which to purchase alcohol. In those days, Papua New Guinea did not have a cash-based economy. Most of the Melanesian people were subsistence farmers, which is to say that they lived off of the food they grew in their own gardens. Their clothes and their houses they made themselves. The natives of Papua New Guinea had no money, and they had no need for it, either, until alcohol went on sale. Then they began to plant coffee beans, and other cash crops, in order to be able to purchase beer.

The abuse of alcohol is a critical problem in Papua New Guinea today. Only a few years ago, there was one chemical dependency counselor in this country of three million people, one treatment center, and a half-dozen A.A. groups.

While I was in Papua New Guinea, I met a Lutheran missionary (himself a recovering alcoholic) who traveled from village to village to educate people about the dangers of alcohol abuse. Actually, he delivered a temperance talk. He carried with him a humble visual aid: a hand-drawn diagram on a piece of cloth, which depicted a man with beer in his belly and a sad face.

There is something deeply ironic about the introduction of alcohol in Papua New Guinea. The same missionaries who transported the story of salvation to the shores of Papua New Guinea also brought with them the devil's brew. I do not mean to denigrate the early missionaries to Papua New Guinea—they worked hard, and made great sacrifices, to bring the Gospel to this country—but it is also true that they influenced the people of Papua New Guinea in a powerful way they could never have anticipated.

The heart of the paradox is this: alcohol often contributes to the destruction of human life—and yet, the wine of Holy Communion is also the substance that conveys Christ to his people. There is a powerful force within the human breast that reaches out for alcohol, for good or for ill. In various time zones of the world—in Papua New Guinea, for one example—the abuse of alcohol is painfully obvious.

107

Tears

"And God himself will be with them;
he will wipe away every tear from their eyes"
(Revelation 21)

It is not unusual for people to shed some tears during their participation in an addictions treatment program.

People who come for treatment, after all, tend to be people in pain. As they begin to get in touch with their feelings, sometimes they cry. When they realize how much they have hurt the people they love, some people weep. Once they get beneath their thick layer of anger, even tough guys can be moved to tears. When people begin to feel grief that they have been avoiding through alcohol or drug-usage or gambling, sometimes their eyes moisten.

When an individual begins to sob, it is common for other people to offer that person a Kleenex. It is a compassionate gesture. It is a reflex. It is a phenomenon I have witnessed many times. As soon as someone begins to experience tears, other people begin to crane their necks, scanning the room for a box of tissues. Once someone has laid hands on the Kleenex box, it is passed swiftly from person to person, until it arrives at the individual in distress.

Many people seem to be uncomfortable around tears. They want to help the person in pain in any way they can, so they hunt for a box of Kleenex with an animated sense of urgency. Before you pass a box of tissues to a person in tears, however, it might be worthwhile to ask yourself whether you are responding to the needs of the person in pain, or to your own needs.

Years ago, when I took some chaplains' training, I was cautioned about offering a box of tissues to a person in tears. "Maybe the person needs to cry," my advisor pointed out to me. "Maybe the person needs to feel those tears on his or her cheek. Maybe it is the only way the person can begin to heal."

It is difficult to sit with someone who is crying. When people hasten to comfort a person in tears with a box of tissues, perhaps they are really seeking to stop the crying, or to deny the hurt. Tears are, fundamentally, about healing and truth. It is not your place or mine to brush away someone else's tears. If a person asks for some tissues, it only makes sense to pass the Kleenex promptly—but unless a person specifically requests a tissue, it may not be an appropriate gesture at all.

In fact, there is a Scripture passage to the effect that it is God who, in due time, "will wipe away every tear from their eyes." It is the Lord's job to wipe away tears, and only when the time is right. Healing for another person may come from God, or it may come from within the person experiencing tears, but it will not come from you or me or from that box of tissues.

That Dawg Don't Hunt

In A.A., people have a sacred right to define a Higher Power in any way that makes sense to them. On one hand, you are welcome to conceive of God or a Higher Power in any way you choose—but, on the other hand, there are some concepts of a Higher Power that probably will not work. Some are simply untenable. Others might deserve to be challenged. Still others are at least worthy of suspicion.

While it is true that you can name your own Higher Power in A.A., I once heard a very different saying from an older Texan which also seems to have a ring of truth: "That dawg don't hunt!" I am inclined to think that the good old boys and the good old gals at A.A. could appreciate the concise wisdom inherent in this phrase: "That dawg don't hunt!"

Here are some examples of "dawgs that don't hunt":

1) Maybe it goes without saying, but you would not want to identify *yourself* as a Higher Power. The Second Step clearly rules out this option: "Came to believe that a Power <u>greater</u> <u>than</u> <u>ourselves</u> could restore us to sanity."

2) Common sense would also eliminate alcohol or drugs as a desirable Higher Power. People's lives sometimes are ruled by these chemicals, but no one would willingly name them as a Higher Power.

3) Another thing that probably will not work as a Higher Power is whatever-you-used-the-last-time-you-were-in-treatment. If a woman has been in treatment four times, and each time maintains that her Higher Power is Jesus, it is apparent that something is wanting. As the saying goes: "If nothing changes, nothing changes."

4) Many people identify their Higher Power as God, but hopefully not as an *angry* God. If you conceive of God as a divine being who is wrathful or punitive, or even indifferent, this God is not likely to be of any help to you in your recovery. Step Three expressly refers to "the <u>care</u> of God as we understood Him." However you might construe God, it will need to be as a benevolent figure.

5) Sometimes people confuse the notion of a Higher Power with some *diversion* from drinking or drug-using. Some profess that their motorcycle or their golf game will keep them sober. It is important to understand that a Higher Power is not a substitute for drinking.

6) You might designate another person as your Higher Power. If you have found someone you trust at an A.A. meeting, you could think of this person as a Higher Power. An A.A. sponsor might be considered a Higher Power, but probably not a family member. If a family member has tried everything possible to keep a loved one from drinking in the past, why should the recovering alcoholic expect to be able to lean on the same family member for sobriety in the future?

7) Could a deceased relative or friend be considered a Higher Power? Could one pray to a deceased person for assistance? Once again, if it has not helped you in the past to pray to a deceased person for assistance, it probably will not help in the future, either.

8) Sometimes people speak of their Higher Power in terms of a doorknob, or a toaster, or a light bulb. When folks identify their Higher Power with an inanimate object, they are stressing that you can call your Higher Power by any name you choose, but I question whether these objects can actually help a person stay sober. If you tell

111

me your Higher Power is a doorknob, and you stay sober, I say, "Good for you!" If you tell me your Higher Power is a doorknob, and you relapse, then you probably need to reconsider your idea of a Higher Power.

9) Can *nature* be regarded as a Higher Power? I knew a Native American man who claimed his Higher Power was an eagle. Nature can be construed as a Higher Power, although this enters into the realm of pantheism and animism.

10) Some people have described their Higher Power as their *courage* or their *conscience*. I myself am suspicious of people who label inner attributes as their Higher Power. When a man claims his Higher Power is his *courage*, is he really talking about his "will power"? Nevertheless, the literature of A.A. sometimes does speak of internal entities—like *conscience*—as a viable Higher Power.[72]

I am reminded of a recovering alcoholic who claimed that he really did not know how to describe his Higher Power. He said that he would go to meetings, talk to his sponsor, and take things one day at a time. He figured that Something must be working for him, although he could not say exactly what it was.

In the end, you may not have to specify the nature of your Higher Power in order to work the A.A. program. If you do try to conceptualize your Higher Power, however, it is important to remember that "some dawgs don't hunt."

The Anatomy of a Grief Letter

"...when pain is to be borne, a little courage helps
more than much knowledge, a little human sympathy
more than much courage, and the least tincture of the
love of God more than all." (C.S. Lewis[73])

Many people who come to treatment for their chemical
dependency or compulsive gambling seem to have had some
significant losses during their lives. Frequently, these patients are
assigned to participate in a "grief group," so they can begin to
cope with their losses while they are undergoing treatment for
their addictions.

The most obvious sort of loss would be the death of a family
member or friend. There are other types of losses that might
trigger the grieving process—a divorce, the loss of a job, the
death of a pet, the loss of health, an abortion or miscarriage, or
even the inability to drink or gamble any more—but I shall focus
on the grief associated with the death of a loved one here, in the
interest of keeping the discussion linear.

(Without launching into detail, it is worth noting that dealing
with chemical dependency or compulsive gambling in itself can
be regarded as grief work.)

The grief groups at a treatment center are intended to help
people unravel the grief issues which so often seem to
accompany addictions. I am not acquainted with any Bible
verses or other magic words which assuage grief
instantaneously, but I have noticed that sometimes it helps
patients to talk about their losses with one another. In some
cases, the healing process can begin when people simply listen to
other people's accounts of their own losses.

After people have had the opportunity to dialogue about their
particular losses, some are invited to write something called a
"grief letter"—which amounts to putting your feelings and
thoughts in writing to the deceased person. The goal of this

exercise, and the end of the grief process itself, is *acceptance* of the loss.

When I recommend that a patient compose a grief letter, I usually suggest that the missive include at least these three elements:

1) *Feelings.* What emotions come to you when you think of the loved one who has died? Sadness? Loneliness? Anger? Guilt? Love? Gratitude? I encourage people to articulate their feelings in their grief letter.

2) *Any connection between the loss and what is going on now in life.* A teenaged drug addict, for example, might acknowledge that he started using drugs more heavily after his mother died from cancer. A compulsive gambler might admit that she took her grief to a casino after her husband perished in a car accident. If people can identify their demise into addiction with a certain loss, it might be helpful to discuss this in the grief letter.

3) *Letting go of the negatives.* When people add the element of "letting go" to their grief letters, it does not mean "forgetting about" the deceased person, for you will never forget someone who was truly important to you. Rather, the idea of "letting go" suggests releasing the negative feelings, that is, saying whatever you need to say in order to relinquish guilt or anger. If you never had the opportunity to say "goodbye" or "I love you" before someone passed away, you could include this in a grief letter, also.

Many patients report that writing a grief letter can be a "wrenching" and emotional experience in itself, and yet, I usually encourage them to read their grief letter to some other people, as well. Some people resist this, of course, for reasons that are understandable. Some will protest that they prefer to read their grief letter at the graveside, and while I would never insist that a grieving person read the grief letter to others, I strongly recommend it.

When you read a grief letter alone at the side of a grave, you might feel intensely alone. The truth is that your loved one is not really there at the grave. On the other hand, your loved one might be more present amidst a group of caring people than at the grave itself.

Grief is a profound issue for many people who come to treatment. A grief letter is a powerful tool for dealing with this issue.

The Angel and the Tour Guide

I remember a day when I went for a walk with my son. At the time, he was one-and-a-half.

My son did not possess a vocabulary yet, but he was an effective communicator. He pointed to his coat on the hook, he jabbed his finger towards the door, and then started making what I would describe as *yearning* sounds. He made his wish known. We haggled about whether he could go outside in his stocking feet, or whether he would wear boots, but we finally did make it outside together.

It was a sunny Saturday in February; the wind was brisk in the open areas. I was thinking in terms of strolling for a few blocks, but this man-child of mine had more ambitious plans in mind.

My son could not form any words at the time, as I mentioned, but he did point to items of interest, made eye-contact with me, and then emitted an urgent "Eh-eh." First, he spotted a squashed Pepsi can in the street. "Eh-eh." Then he noticed the yellow sign with the black arrow pointing upward. "Eh-eh-eh." He called attention to the black plastic tubing in the ditch, too. "Eh-eh-eh-eh."

For some reason, the lad liked to pull his stocking cap down so it almost covered his eyes. My parental instinct was to pull up on his cap so that his vision was unhindered—but this was my agenda, not his. He voiced his irritation, and then slid his cap down to eye-level once again.

We listened to the gurgle of a little stream that issued from a culvert. Further down the street, we heard the hum of the wires near the electric plant. We studied the brown mutt that barked at us from behind the chain-link fence.

On we trudged: down the hill, across the bridge, and then left on Main Street. We covered about a mile, I would estimate—the tour guide and the guardian angel.

116

Periodically, I would slide his stocking cap above his eyebrows, so the kid could see! He, in turn, would fuss, and tug it back down again.

They say that spirituality is about the things you *notice*. You can focus upon your worries and your frustrations (everyone has some, you know) and the painful things of the past. Or, you could go for a walk when it is sunny, with your boy, if you have one. You can train your attention upon the negative aspects of life—if you want to do so—or you can enjoy some of the little things along the way.

It seems as though God lets people decide for themselves what they want to notice: the troubling things or the blessings. God allows folks to dwell upon whatever they will—but children do not. Children simply demand your attention. They seize it! "Eh-eh-eh!" One way or another, children will get you to notice them.

Long ago I learned it was futile for me to attempt to talk to my wife as soon as I got home from work. My young sons would not permit this. I was required to pay attention to them first, even if only for two minutes. After I had acknowledged them, and only then, I was allowed to converse with their mother.

Spirituality is about what you notice, and children boldly lay claim to your attention.

I remember the tale of a man who was a recovering alcoholic. He recalled that he emerged from his house one morning, but came to a halt on his front step. He stared at the evergreen on his lawn. He remembered planting the tree as a seedling 10 years before, but he had never realized that it had grown—until that very moment. Now, the tree stood a glorious 15 feet tall. It occurred to the man that he did not notice the tree while it was growing up, not back in his drinking days. It occurred to the man that he had never noticed his own children growing up, either.

"Eh-eh-eh."

117

As for my little guy, he "petered out" after we had walked that mile. I ended up carrying him home...uphill...asleep. I did not mind bearing him home in my arms, either.

And to think that I was trying so hard to uncover <u>his</u> eyes.

The Church is My Mother

I remember listening to a nun, who was a friend of mine, as she poured out her bitterness about the Catholic Church. She recited her litany of complaints about what she perceived as ridiculous rules, slush-for-brains superiors, pig-headed parishioners, and other assorted injustices she claimed she had endured during her life in the church.

After listening to her diatribe for a while, I asked her why she did not just leave her religious order, why she did not simply walk away from it all. She shot back at me disgustedly, "Because the church is my mother!"

I suppose I remember this conversation for the richness of her reply. There does seem to be something profound about the metaphor she chose: "The church is my mother."

The truth is that there is something about the church that attracts criticism and scorn. For some reason, the church functions as a magnet for people's grievances, petty or otherwise. Perhaps the church is held up to some unrealistic expectations— or maybe the church is simply not what it ought to be. In either case, it does not require much depth of insight to identify the shortcomings of the church; the average seventh grader could probably mount a cogent critique against the Lady we know as the church.

Some people seem to get angry at the church, and stay angry, even for life. Others just cling to a perpetual sense of disillusionment about the church. I do not intend to criticize the church or apologize for it, either—but I will say that something rings true about my feminine friend's words: "The church is my mother."

One rather common complaint I have heard from those who profess to be disaffected with the church is that, "It was forced down my throat when I was a kid" (which is indeed a violent image when you stop to think about it). It is interesting that folks never seem to complain about being forced to go to grade school

119

when they were children, but this is beside the point. It does seem that the authority of the church tends to converge with the authority of our parents. At some point, the two become indistinguishable.

One powerful way to rebel against parental authority is to oppose your parents' religion. Could it all be as simple as this? Those who exhibit defiance or contempt towards the church are still struggling to free themselves from the influence of their parents?

If you go back a generation or two, parenting involved a lot of shaming techniques—and the church only reflected the shame-based approach to parenting that was found in so many homes. If the church represents parental authority for a great many people, it follows that resentment towards the church is traceable to dear old Mom and Pop, and the way they ran their household.

The task of dealing with resentment against the church is no different from the challenge to redress any ill-will towards your parents. How do you let go of resentment towards your parents, but by working towards acceptance? How do you get rid of old anger for your mother or father but by asking yourself, honestly, whether you think they did the best they could? Part of the process of growing up is learning to forgive your parents.

So it is with the church, too. Coming to terms with the church just might involve acceptance, growing up, and acknowledging that she (the church) did the best she could with what she had.

I once heard a speaker make this striking claim: "For the most part, our parents were heroic people." As my mind plays across this sentence, I come to a halt at the word *heroic*. It sounds extreme. My parents, *heroic*? No, Willie Mays was heroic. Mother Teresa was heroic. Abraham Lincoln was heroic—but my parents? Heroic? My mother the church? Heroic?

In the sense that they did the best that they knew how, my parents were heroic people, and so were yours. The church is an easy prey for criticism, but there is also something beautiful about that Old Woman the church. There is something honorable about her.

I am confident that some of you who read these words will not come to the same conclusions about the church that I have reached, which is okay, I guess. I myself find some solace, however, in the thought that the church is my mother. The notion of *mother* suggests indebtedness or obligation, among other things that cause me to squirm—but the metaphor of *mother* also calls for acceptance, plain and simple. After all, there is something heroic about her.

Gregory P. Gabriel

The Empty Pew

One summer, my family passed through Springfield, Illinois on our vacation. While in Springfield, we took the opportunity to visit the tomb of Abraham Lincoln, the house in which he lived for 17 years, and Lincoln's law office. We also made a stop at First Presbyterian Church, which advertises its possession of the Lincoln family church pew. The host at the church showed us the famous Lincoln pew, and then explained that Lincoln's wife and sons frequently came to worship services in Springfield, but that Mr. Lincoln himself rarely occupied the pew that is identified with his name. It seems that Abraham Lincoln was not a church-goer.

Many people who come to treatment for chemical dependency or compulsive gambling seem to have difficulties with the church. So did the sixteenth president of the United States.

I once read a biography about Lincoln—*Abraham Lincoln: Redeemer President* by Allen C. Guelzo. This monograph comments on Lincoln's struggles with faith. When Lincoln was 25, he wrote an angry book which denied the veracity of the Scriptures and the divinity of Christ. Lincoln intended to publish this book, but a friend—who feared the political repercussions of such a book—convinced Lincoln to commit the manuscript to the fire. Some of Lincoln's antagonism for religion moderated as he passed into middle age, but he remained a religious skeptic all of his life.

Mr. Lincoln seemed to know the Bible rather well—indeed, he frequently quoted it in his political speeches—but he also acknowledged candidly that he was not a Christian. He stated that he wanted to be a believer, but could not bring himself to be one. Lincoln did seem to have some convictions about providence and even predestination, but he could not bring himself to believe in a God who loved him personally.

122

I was curious whether Lincoln ever was baptized, so I sent an e-mail to the author of this book. The Lincoln scholar replied, "It is unlikely that he was baptized."

It is very difficult to assess the faith of another human being—especially one I have met only in the pages of history books. Nevertheless, I shall venture to point out that Lincoln's mother died from milk sickness when he was nine. Many people who have suffered a serious loss have a hard time with religious faith. The author of this book repeatedly notes Lincoln's keen sensitivity to any form of desertion. Abraham Lincoln also experienced the deaths of his sister, his fiancée, and two of his sons. If Lincoln had a hard time trusting in a loving God, it would be understandable.

Lincoln also had a troubled relationship with his father. Many people who have serious difficulties with a parent also seem to struggle with God and religion. Lincoln did not invite his father to his wedding. He did not attend his father's funeral, nor did he provide a stone for his father's grave for years after his father's death. It is hard to know exactly what the problem was between Lincoln and his father, but witnesses remember that Lincoln's father used to knock him down when he was a boy. Lincoln's father, who was illiterate, did not approve of his son's habit of reading, either. Lincoln viewed his father as a subsistence farmer without ambition to better himself. Lincoln's parents were staunch Calvinist Baptists, but Lincoln himself resisted affiliation with any church. Perhaps Lincoln's struggle with the church had something to do with his struggle with his father.

Lincoln was a very logical man. He had the well-honed intellect of an attorney. Some say that he wanted to believe in God, but that reason kept getting in the way. Some people who come to treatment for addictions cannot quite find God, either, because they are unable (in treatment jargon) "to get out of their heads."

When people in treatment have a hard time with God or the church, I do not attempt to engage them in theological discourse.

Rather, I ask, "What kinds of important losses have you experienced?" Or, I invite them to tell me about their fathers. Sometimes I encourage them to be less analytical and more trusting. These are some approaches to potential spiritual progress. They may or may not fill empty church pews.

The Greater Challenge

One of the great heroes in American history was Meriwether Lewis. Together with William Clark and a crew of about 30, he traversed the North American continent in 1804-06. Lewis was commissioned by President Jefferson to explore the North American continent in order to determine whether it was possible to cross the entire continent by water. I read about the adventures of Lewis and his intrepid crew in a book called *Undaunted Courage* by Stephen A. Ambrose.

During their epic journey, Lewis and his party struggled valiantly against all sorts of adversity—from powerful river currents to being lost in the wilderness; from mountain ranges to swarms of mosquitoes; from hunger to grizzly bears. They also encountered challenges related to alcohol. Indeed, the problem of alcohol abuse is woven right into the tale of this heroic odyssey:

❑ Captain Lewis hired a boat contractor in Pittsburgh to build a 55-foot keelboat for the expedition. The boat-builder was a heavy drinker, however, and therefore could not complete the job on schedule. This delayed the start of the expedition by six weeks.

❑ Lewis decided to take a physician from Philadelphia along on the trip. The doctor literally missed the boat, however, probably because he was drunk. (Imagine missing out on the Lewis and Clark expedition because you were intoxicated!)

❑ In the early stages of the journey, Lewis' own men would either sneak off and get drunk, or break into the expedition's supply of whiskey. On one occasion, two of the enlisted men on the expedition got drunk—while one was supposed to be on guard duty—and as a consequence, were sentenced to be flogged.

The author notes that Lewis and his crew set out on their adventure with 120 gallons of whiskey, which was given to the soldiers in daily rations. This supply was not intended to be enough to last the entire journey, but just enough to get the men far out into the wilderness, so that they could not turn back. The problems associated with alcohol did seem to disappear, too, as the group ventured further into the wilderness, where there was no alcohol to be had.

When Lewis and his party made their triumphant return to the east, however, the issue of alcohol abuse returned with a vengeance. At first, Lewis and the others were the toast of eastern society, but within three years of his homecoming, Lewis had lost control of his drinking. He was depressed, and unhappy about being unable to find a wife; both problems were exacerbated by his return to drinking. At the age of 35, Meriwether Lewis took his own life.

Lewis had experienced problems with his drinking as a younger man. At the age of 21, well before his legendary voyage into the wilderness, Lewis had been court-martialed for getting drunk and challenging an officer to a dual.

When Lewis and his expedition finally reached the Pacific Ocean, one might expect that Lewis would have been jubilant, but there is no suggestion of his elation in his journal. Ambrose speculates that his subdued reaction was that of an alcoholic deprived of alcohol: "Whatever Lewis's emotional state, it was strongly affected by his drinking habits." Ambrose adds, "It had been a long time since Meriwether Lewis had had a drink. And the certainty was that it would be a long time before he had another."[74]

When his trials in the wilderness came to an end, Lewis had to face a challenge of a different sort—namely, his drinking problem. For all of the adversity he overcame in the wild, Lewis seems to have lost his struggle with alcohol.

People often speak of spirituality in terms of a journey. Meriwether Lewis was the hero of the most celebrated journey in American history—yet somehow, he lost his way on his own inner journey. "Recovery" is all about this inner journey. The saga of Meriwether Lewis poses an intriguing question: Which journey is more arduous? A bold venture into the wilderness—facing grizzly bears and treacherous mountain passes—or facing your own addictions, your own demons, your own life? Which challenge really is the greater?

Gregory P. Gabriel

The Incarnation

The Christmas season is, fundamentally, a celebration of the *Incarnation*. The word Incarnation is a theological term which refers to the revealing of God in human form. The root of the word Incarnation would be *carn*, which refers to *flesh (*just as a *carn*ivore would be a *flesh* eater*)*. When God makes himself known in human flesh, as a tiny baby born in Bethlehem, this is the Incarnation. John's Gospel summarizes the Christmas story in this sweet sentence: "The word became flesh and dwelt among us." The Incarnation of Christ is the miracle at the core of Christmas. It connotes the nearness and the reality of God.

Bill W. had a friend named Father Ed Dowling, who was a Jesuit priest from St. Louis. Father Dowling was an admirer of the A.A. fellowship. He once made a particularly insightful observation about the A.A. program: He drew an analogy between the A.A. program and the Incarnation.[75]

There does seem to be something downright incarnational about A.A. Sometimes God seems especially real to people at an A.A. meeting. Sometimes the love of God becomes tangible in a treatment program where the 12-Step philosophy is espoused.

I happen to think that A.A. helps to *flesh out* the theology of the church. It is not enough just to talk about forgiveness, as we often do in the church. In A.A., one really has to deal with resentment in order to maintain sobriety. In the sense that A.A. manages to put some *flesh* on the bones of Christian theology, there is something incarnational about A.A.

In order to illustrate further how A.A. can be said to be incarnational, I enlist the support of two other clergymen who were supportive of A.A. back in the 1930's and 1940's. Dr. Samuel Shoemaker was an Episcopal priest who was credited with teaching Bill W. and Dr. Bob many of the spiritual principles later embodied in A.A. Dr. Shoemaker once made this concise observation about how people achieve sobriety:

> "We lean first on another human being who seems to be finding the answer, and then we lean on the higher Power that stands behind him."[76]

In other words, we find God in and through other people.

This incarnational thought happens to summarize my approach to working as a chaplain in the field of addictions. I really have no interest in idle discussions with patients about theological abstractions (e.g. what God looks like). If they want to get in touch with God or spirituality, I recommend that they start by trusting another human being.

Dr. Harry Fosdick was a clergyman who wrote a positive review of the Big Book in the early years of the A.A. program. Bill W. once referred to him as "the very first clergyman to recognize" A.A.[77] Fosdick, too, seemed to discover something incarnational about A.A. He was impressed by the vestiges of the love of God he encountered at A.A. gatherings. Fosdick states:

> "I have listened to many learned arguments about God, but for honest-to-goodness experiential evidence of God, His power personally appropriated and His reality indubitably assured, give me a good meeting of A.A.!"[78]

Each of these clergymen who witnessed the formative years of A.A. noticed something incarnational about the fellowship of A.A. During the Christmas season, we celebrate the Incarnation of Christ, and we also give thanks for recovery through A.A., where, in a sense, God also is incarnate.

Gregory P. Gabriel

The Legitimate Use of the Word "Spiritual"

One of the most overworked and under-appreciated words in the English language might be the term *spirit*. A number of related words—*spirited, spiritual,* and *spirituality*—all seem to get used in ways which range from casual to crass. And yes, this rankles me.

- ❑ When we speak of a *spirited* horse, we are describing an animal which rears up on its hind legs and lashes the air with its hooves. Here the word *spirited* means spunky or half-wild, I guess. I suppose this would be an innocuous use of the term.

- ❑ I once read a newspaper article which described a certain defensive tackle as the *spiritual* leader of his football team. In this context, I assume that the word *spiritual* means fiery or inspirational. This strikes me as a rather trivial use of the term spiritual.

- ❑ I remember seeing an advertisement for a casino, which featured this slogan: "Feel the Spirit—Live the Excitement." In this instance, the word *spirit* refers to the action at the black jack tables or the adventure of the slot machines. Let us call this use of the word *spirit* "deceptive."

My point is that the word *spirit* (and all of its variations) sometimes gets used in ways which seem mundane, or even downright illegitimate. On the other hand, I like the way the French employ the word *spirit* in the expression *esprit de corps*, which refers to the enthusiasm of members of a group for one another, or for the group's purposes. I believe that the factor which unites people at an A.A. or G.A. meeting is a common bond of suffering—an *esprit de corps.* Now *there* is the proper use of the word *spirit.*

For all of my musings on the word *spirit*, however, I doubt that many people have gained a greater sense of spirituality from dwelling on the word itself. The precise definition of the word spirituality is probably not as important as an appreciation of its connotation. In a fundamental way, spirituality is about relationships—relationships with God, and other people, and with ourselves. When we become honest with ourselves, open to other people, and willing to do whatever God wants us to do—this is spirituality. This is the *esprit de corps* of the 12-Step program.

I am going to let Bill W. have the last word on the subject of spirituality: "We find that no one need have difficulty with the spirituality of the program. *Willingness, honesty and open mindedness are the essentials of recovery. But these are indispensable.*"[79]

Gregory P. Gabriel

The Man Who Would Not Hurry

Once upon a time, I encountered a portly old fellow with dazzling white hair and a full white beard. He had a gentle way about him. To tell you the truth, he reminded me of Santa Claus in civilian wear. Whenever he laughed, I noticed that his entire body shook, like, well, a bowl full of jelly.

Although he was a merry sort, he suddenly became very solemn when he began to talk about his own journey to sobriety. His eyes narrowed and his demeanor turned serious as he prepared to reveal what he considered one of the cardinal rules of A.A. This rule is not written down anywhere, he noted ominously, "But if you want to stay sober, you don't drive over 55 miles per hour."

"You don't drive 57, and you don't drive 56," he warned. "If you value your sobriety, you will keep your speedometer nailed to 55."

I was taken aback by his sudden display of severity. I mean, what is the big deal? Doesn't everybody exceed the speed limit? What is so crucial about keeping your speed down to 55? I do not think that even the state troopers stay within the 55 mph speed limit, do they?

The man did not make any effort to explain himself. Perhaps he wanted to let his listeners figure it out for themselves. What is so all-fired important about holding your car down to 55 on the highway?

As I considered his odd counsel, it occurred to me that people probably do get into "hurry-up" thinking when they surpass the posted speed limit. When folks knowingly exceed the posted speed limit, perhaps it does breed guilt. If you are driving 67 mph in a 55 mph zone, you know that you could be pulled over by the highway patrol and ticketed. There would seem to be something vaguely dangerous about consciously doing something illegal. Ignoring the speed limit may well foster the thinking that "rules-are-for-other-people."

This man made his point rather sternly, but I could begin to understand what speeding might have to do with sobriety. A lot of people seem to find that recovery has something to do with learning to observe limits, and that spirituality has something to do with slowing down.

This calls to mind a story from John's Gospel, chapter 11. It seems that Mary and Martha sent word to Jesus that their brother Lazarus (who was a close friend to Jesus) was gravely ill. In fact, he was dying. Most likely, these women expected this great healer to rush to the rescue of Lazarus—but he did not rush at all.

When Jesus learned that his friend was near death, he did arise and respond to the situation...after two days. After two days? You mean to say that Jesus waited two full days before he reacted to a life-or-death situation?

After waiting around for 48 hours, as the story goes, Jesus did set out for Bethany, where he found that Lazarus was already dead. Jesus eventually brought Lazarus back to life.

Now, the thing that strikes me about this story is that Jesus did not hurry. As a matter of fact, I cannot think of any story in the New Testament which suggests that Jesus ever acted in haste. Can you imagine a person who never hurried? Sometimes he did things immediately, and sometimes he did first-things-first, but I do not think that Jesus ever hurried.

Tell me one more time: What was the reason you reserve the right to exceed the speed limit? It seems to me that sobriety has something to do with regarding limits, and that spirituality has something to do with slowing down. I do not know whether you fancy yourself a religious person or a spiritual person, but it seems to me that neither Jesus nor Santa was one to hurry.

The Meeting in the Basement

They still hold Al-Anon meetings in the basement of the old Methodist church down the street.

On any given night, I suppose there are thousands of A.A. and Al-Anon meetings going on in the bowels of churches across the country. Somehow, the basement of a church seems like an appropriate place for such a meeting, too.

As you walk through the side door of that stately old church, you are confronted with a fundamental choice between two staircases: the ascending stairs lead to the nave of the church, while the other leads to the basement. If you follow the descending steps, you arrive at the room where the Al-Anon meeting convenes. It is the room with the coffeepot and the well-worn couch. I believe that the Al-Anon group meets in a room that is directly beneath the altar area of the church—which somehow seems fitting.

A.A. and Al-Anon have always been "underground" organizations, in more ways than one. These basement meetings have always been predicated on the principle of anonymity. The gathering upstairs, by contrast, is not governed by confidentiality. There is little that is secretive about the proceedings of the church, but A.A. is an underground movement.

A.A. is an evening fellowship. I am aware that some A.A. and Al-Anon groups do assemble at noon or even in the morning, but it is still predominately a night-time community. The meeting upstairs is different, however. "The early morning belongs to the Church of the Risen Christ," writes Dietrich Bonhoeffer (a Lutheran pastor).[80] The church's worship is illuminated by sunlight through stained glass, but the meeting in the basement prefers a different sort of lighting. A.A. and Al-Anon meetings commonly come together after dark and underground.

134

Conversation flows freely at those meetings in the cellar. Folks seem to come to life below the surface of the earth. Maybe they feel more comfortable there. The atmosphere upstairs is just not the same. I think that people feel more constrained in the church proper. As a parish pastor, I have endured the chilly silence of congregational meetings held in the nave of the church. People seem to have the idea that you are supposed to hush up and sit still when sitting in the pews upstairs.

If A.A. is an underground society, then the church is the meeting upstairs.

If you suspect that this comparison of A.A. and the church is leading to the conclusion that one is superior to the other, you are mistaken. Each has its own place: the church meets at the top of the stairs, and the Al-Anon group gathers in the basement. I become annoyed when I hear A.A. people disparaging the church, especially those who have never tried to exercise leadership in the church. On the other hand, I get peeved when church folks suggest that there is something inadequate about A.A. or Al-Anon.

Both A.A. and the church have their place: one at the bottom of the stairs, and one at the top.

When I looked up the word "symbiosis" in my dictionary, I found a picture of a tiny bird atop a hippopotamus. In this case, I gather that the bird pecks bugs off the hippo's neck while the hippo, in turn, gives the bird a free ride. You get the idea, anyway. Symbiosis is when two organisms cooperate to their mutual advantage.

When I consider the relationship between A.A. and the church, I am not sure which might represent the hippo and which one the bird, but I like the idea of symbiosis. A.A. and the church are indebted to one another. There is no reason they cannot respect each other, and rely upon each other, like the hippo and the bird.

The A.A. movement grew out of a non-denominational Christian fellowship called the Oxford Group. One observer compared the early A.A. organization to "first-century

135

Christianity."[81] (It is interesting to note that the early Christians in Rome met in the catacombs—secretively and underground.)

On the other hand, the church also depends upon A.A. for help in dealing with alcoholism. A.A. and Al-Anon push at the edges of the church's comprehension of spirituality.

As I see it, A.A. and the church seem to complement each other. It is just that one meets upstairs and the other in the basement.

The Spirit or the Spirits?

There is a holy day on the calendar of the church that is known as the day of Pentecost. Pentecost is a festival day that remembers a time when the Spirit of God was poured out upon the disciples of Christ. I happen to be a member of a denomination which seldom talks about the Spirit, except on this day.

According to the Book of Acts, the second chapter, the Spirit was manifest in a dramatic way at Pentecost. There was a tremendous surge of wind; there were tongues of fire dancing above the disciples' heads; and the disciples themselves engaged in some sort of ecstatic speech, which everyone, even visitors from distant lands, could understand as if it were their own native tongue.

Evidently, some bystanders did not notice the mighty wind or the flames, but they were aware that something amazing had come upon the disciples. Others who were present that day took a more cynical view of it all, and said of the disciples, "They are filled with new wine." When overcome by the Spirit, the disciples became so gleeful and exuberant and uninhibited that some onlookers assumed that they were drunk. The truth, of course, is that they were intoxicated with the Spirit.

It is interesting to think that it might be difficult to distinguish between people who are filled with the Spirit and people who are inebriated with alcohol. You might suppose that the two would be polar opposites—spirituality and drunkenness—but they are not.

(Jesus himself was a Spirit-filled man who was mistaken for a drunkard. You could look it up. Luke 7:34.)

There is something intriguing about the comparison between the word *spirit* and the word *spirits*.[82]

The term *spirit* comes from the Latin word *spiritus*, which literally means *breath*. The spirit is the breath of life within a person; it is that which enlivens a person, or that which animates.

137

The story of Pentecost recounts the day when there came from the heavens a Great Breath. It was the Spirit of God, and the disciples clearly were animated by this Spirit.

A curious thing happens when the word *spirit* is used in its plural form, however. The term *spirits* often refers to alcoholic beverages. How come the word *spirit* suggests the very breath of God, but *spirits* is booze? Is it any wonder that the bystanders were confused at Pentecost? They could not discern whether the disciples were under the influence of the Spirit or the spirits.

Often, the two are interchanged unwittingly. Theologically speaking, I suppose that an alcoholic would be someone who puts alcohol in the place in his or her life that rightly belongs to God. Alcoholism might be described as the pathological substitution of the spirits for the Spirit.

Someone once observed that alcoholics do tend to be spiritual people. You would have to be a spiritual sort of person to commit yourself so completely to a singular object of devotion. The fatal mistake that characterizes the disease of alcoholism, however, is the tendency to replace the Spirit with spirits.

If we all were filled with the Spirit, I suppose that we all might carry on as deliriously and demonstratively as the disciples at Pentecost. Being a reserved individual of northern European descent, however, I think I shall settle for a smaller serving of the Spirit. I would be satisfied if God granted me enough of the Spirit to accept the things I cannot change, and enough breath to make it through the day.

The Tractor Man

Some years ago, I lived in a hamlet in Nebraska. The village consisted of a handful of houses, a Lutheran church, a basement beauty shop, and a miniature post office that was open every day (except Sunday) from 8-10 a.m. Main Street was paved, but the other street was not. I lived in the parsonage on Main Street.

I was raking leaves in my front yard one Saturday morning, when I heard from behind me the unmistakable "PUTT-putt-putt-putt" of a "B" John Deere. I turned and beheld a grizzled old fellow on a green tractor. He wore a gray parka and a seed-corn cap pulled down to his eyebrows. He had a severe expression on his face; maybe it was determination. The man cruised past me without even a glance, chasing the leaves in the street as he drove. He appeared to be headed towards the post office at the other end of the street.

I stood watching him for a while. The man was a striking figure. He even seemed vaguely familiar.

I was told, later, that this fellow was called "Smokey," because he had had a lively fastball in his younger years. They said that he lived about two miles south of town, and that he made his run to the post office every morning, rain or shine. Folks claimed that he had lost his driver's license many years ago—the same time he crashed his pickup into a light pole—so now he made his way around on that antique John Deere.

People remembered that his wife and children had gotten fed up with his drinking and his temper, and had moved away from him a long time ago. Smokey lived off of the largesse of others: he stayed in a farmhouse for free, although he did mow the yard. Someone else brought him groceries.

He was, at the same time, a comical figure and a tragic one—tooling into town each morning to fetch his mail. Smokey even made his mail run on his rickety old tractor in the dead of winter, clattering down Main Street and bursting

139

heroically through the snowdrifts. Sometimes I wondered what was so desperately important about getting the mail. I could not believe that he kept up a lively correspondence with anyone.

Smokey was an odd fellow, and yet, somehow I sensed that I knew him.

This man was more than just an eccentric old bird. He was an archetype. He was a Tractor Man.

A tractor is a symbol of power, of brute force, of the will to go forward. The man astride that John Deere was a metaphor for an ego that will not be denied. A Tractor Man is one who will not yield, or one who cannot.

Dr. Harry Tiebout was a psychiatrist and a friend of Alcoholics Anonymous in the early years of the movement. He studied alcoholics, and the factors that brought them to the point of surrender. Tiebout observed: "...the act of surrender...is an unconscious event, not willed by the patient even if he should desire to do so."[83] An alcoholic, in other words, cannot choose to capitulate. A Tractor Man cannot dismount from his machine of his own accord, not even if he wants to do so—not without some help, not without some influence of the divine.

I figure that no one really knows how chemical dependency treatment works. There is a great deal of mystery about how and why people surrender. Treatment is a combination of the elements that sometimes enable people to descend from their tractors: abstinence, compassion, confrontation, acceptance, focus on feelings, review of chemical usage, and respectful treatment (to name a few of them).

Some people manage to climb down from their tractor while in treatment, but others never do.

Perhaps old Smokey reminded me of some other alcoholic I have known, or maybe he reflected my own tractoresque ego.

Whatever the case, Smokey died about a year after I first laid eyes on him. They found him slumped over his kitchen table. People around town remembered that he had always insisted that he wanted to be buried without any ceremony, so they honored his wish. I suppose that old "B" John Deere is rusting out in someone's grove right now.

Finally, the tractor is at rest.

Gregory P. Gabriel

Tight Pants

I was looking for a pair of blue jeans in Penney's one day. The sales clerk, who was a lass of about 19, was attempting to assist me. She asked if I might be interested in the Levi 501's.

Now, the mere mention of Levi 501's instantly brought back to me the slogan from an old television commercial: "Levi 501's—a skotch more room in the seat and thighs." I think that the commercial was intended to appeal to middle-aged men who might appreciate more spacious trousers, but I stiffened at the suggestion of Levi 501's.

I turned and stared at her. Maybe my eyes even narrowed. What was that remark supposed to mean? When she mentioned Levi 501's, was she implying that I could use a skotch more room in the seat and thighs of my pants? Why? Because I am aging and losing my manly physique, and soon will be jacking my pants up around my chest? Was she rendering the opinion that I was ready for some baggier bottoms? Levi 501's! Indeed!

I studied her fresh face for a moment, trying to detect whether she intended to ridicule me, but the young woman only stared back at me blankly, as if to ask, "What?"

I decided that she meant no insult by her question. Heck, she probably was not old enough to remember the television commercial anyway. It did occur to me, however, that I felt threatened by the encouragement to try some more abundant britches. The suggestion that I might be in need of such grace came to me as an affront.

This reminds me of another tale about tight pants, an anecdote that was related to me by the wife of an alcoholic. The woman told me that her husband, who was about 50, never cared for shopping. In fact, she bought all of his clothes for him. For some reason, however, he came home with a pair of blue jeans that he claimed to have picked out for himself.

When she examined his purchase, she read the label, and laughed out loud. He had bought a pair of pants with a 32-inch

142

waist. She knew that he could never hitch them around his considerable "beer belly." Obviously, it had been a long time since he had shopped for pants for himself. Gleefully, she recommended that he pass the pants along to their teenaged son.

The man took this as a challenge. Promptly, he began to peel off his pants before her eyes, and then slid his feet into the new trousers with the 32-inch waist. Although it was a struggle, he managed to pull the pants up over his hips. He grimaced as he fastened the snap beneath his paunch. Then, with a mighty hop, he muscled the zipper all the way to the top. Triumphantly, he turned to his wife with his hands on his hips and crowed, "So, you thought they wouldn't fit me, huh?"

He looked so pitiful in those tight pants, his wife remembered, and yet he was so proud. In this fellow's case, his tight-fitting dungarees were a manifestation of his denial—of the effects of his drinking, and perhaps of his own mortality.

I have noticed that men and women in treatment who favor extremely tight-fitting jeans (presumably to enhance their sex appeal) do not seem to do well in recovery. I submit that there is a correlation between tight pants and difficulty in fitting into the A.A. program. Obviously, there is no dress code in A.A., but people in skin-tight jeans seem to have a hard time easing into the program. Tight blue jeans might connote a lot of different things (false pride, being "too big for your britches," being a "tightly wrapped" person) but none is an asset for recovery.

The *Twenty-Four Hours a Day* book recommends that we "wear the world like a loose garment."[84] As I understand this pearl of wisdom, it is not necessarily intended to commend commodious coveralls, but rather to endorse a particular way of living. Wear the world like a loose garment!

It seems to me that spirituality is more closely related to *flexibility* than it is to *constriction*. Spirituality has something to do with our capacity to stretch, to give, and to maneuver freely. Everything in the 12-Step program seems to favor loose-fitting clothing, at least in a figurative sense. Whether or not you decide to go with the Levi 501's, we all could probably use a "skotch more room" in our relationships and in our lives.

Twin Tornadoes

A tornado descended upon a small town, roaring like a freight train. An awesome force shattered windows, ripped rooftops from houses, and sent automobiles tumbling. People huddled in terror in their basements. Some prayed earnestly. Some screamed at the top of their lungs as the violent wind rattled locked doors.

In a matter of seconds, the tornado was gone. People emerged from their hiding places—dazed, shaken, alarmed. They surveyed the wreckage all around them. They inquired about the safety of others. It was a stunning display of nature's savage power.

It occurs to me that a twister is a lot like an addiction.

According to the Big Book, "The alcoholic is like a tornado roaring his way through the lives of others."[85] An addiction to alcohol, drugs, or to gambling—like an F-4 tornado—is something malevolent and chaotic and destructive. An addiction can shred families, topple careers, and wipe out life-savings— like a tornado tearing through a trailer court. Whether you are talking about an addiction or a tornado, it is something "cunning, baffling, powerful."[86]

If you want to know how difficult it is for a person with an addiction to pick up the pieces of his or her life once the addiction has been arrested, take a stroll through a neighborhood that has been devastated by a tornado. The task of cleaning up is absolutely overwhelming. Still, the Big Book enjoins people to start somewhere: "Clear away the wreckage of your past."[87]

One striking difference between a tornado and an addiction, of course, is that the former attracts the attention of the news media in a way that the latter does not. An addiction may well have the cumulative effect of a cyclone, but it does not garner as much press. If the havoc created by an addiction in any given community could somehow be represented visually in an area of 20 square blocks, surely there would be photojournalists on the scene and news helicopters hovering overhead. Certainly people would be in awe of an addiction if they could see its capacity for destruction as clearly as they can examine the aftermath of a tornado.

The subject of tornadoes reminds me of Job in the Old Testament. Job is a man who loses everything he has due to a series of calamities, including a strong wind (tornado?) which brings down the roof of his house. Job struggles with the injustice of his situation, challenging God to explain himself, until God speaks to him from out of a whirlwind (tornado?). Instead of quoting God's exact words to Job, allow me to substitute a poignant question from the Big Book: *"Who are you to say there is no God?"*[88]

A tornado is a humbling experience. It serves as a terrible reminder that we are powerless over many things. It helps people to remember their need to depend upon God. It conjures up a sense of vulnerability in people who might otherwise feel secure about their lives. It causes people to think hard about their priorities.

The Book of Job was originally written in the Hebrew language. In Job, there is a Hebrew word (*ba-rak*) which can be translated either as "to bless" or "to curse." This is an interesting thought: the same event can either be termed a blessing or a curse. An addiction to alcohol or gambling—is it a curse or a blessing? It could be either one. What about a tornado? Is it possible that God could bring something good even from a sickening tragedy like a tornado?

What is a Spiritual Awakening?

"Having had a spiritual awakening as the result of these steps..."
(Step 12)

Members of Alcoholics Anonymous sometimes talk about *spiritual awakenings*. Some people suppose that a spiritual awakening must refer to some kind of dramatic supernatural experience—like the appearance of an angel!—but this is not necessarily what the phrase means. Many A.A. members describe relatively mundane experiences as the moment of their spiritual awakening.

I have spoken with a man who insists that Jesus Christ came to talk to him one afternoon as the man was out walking. I have met a woman who swears that she died on an operating table, visited the next world, and then returned to this life once again. It is not for me to say whether or not their experiences were authentic, but I do know that a spiritual awakening does not have to be anything so incredible.

While some folks claim to have had a spiritual awakening of an earthshaking nature, the majority of A.A. members seem to speak of spiritual awakenings that are comparatively tame. Some statistics which are cited commonly maintain that only 10% of people in recovery will experience a spiritual awakening that is distinctly miraculous, while the other 90% construe a spiritual awakening as something comparatively down-to-earth or subtle.[89]

It is interesting to note that the two founders of the A.A. movement had very different experiences that they considered spiritual awakenings: one had a sudden and intense spiritual awakening, but the other claimed that he never did have a sensational moment-of-truth.

Bill W. was hospitalized for his alcoholism back in 1934 when he experienced a brilliant white light, and a tremendous surge of joy and peace, which he identified with the beginning of his sobriety.[90] The other co-founder of A.A., Dr. Bob, preferred

147

to think that a spiritual awakening came upon him slowly and gradually as he endeavored to be of help to other alcoholics.[91]

Apparently, a spiritual awakening can come as something awesome and powerful, or it can come in a form that is milder. The latter variety seems to be more prevalent.

Bill W. was one who had an amazing experience which he regarded as his spiritual awakening, and yet he wrote in the Big Book that spiritual awakenings do not have to be anything "in the nature of sudden and spectacular upheavals."[92] In a brief addendum to the Big Book, he describes a spiritual awakening as "the personality change sufficient to bring about recovery from alcoholism."[93]

He alludes to spiritual awakenings of the "educational variety"—presumably, which would include the times when you gain some new information about yourself, or the moment in which you figure out a novel way to address an old problem. When people learn how to let go of a deep resentment, or when they discover in themselves a new-found maturity or compassion for others, it could be described as their spiritual awakening.

Bill W. acknowledges that spiritual awakenings often steal upon a person slowly, indeed, that other people might be aware of your spiritual awakening before you yourself even realize it.

Bill W. refers to a spiritual awakening as "a profound alteration in [one's] reaction to life."[94] A spiritual awakening might be an experience that is spectacular or jarring, or it may be something as unremarkable as a seed of humility that slowly but surely takes root in a person. It seems to me that the important thing about a spiritual awakening—whether it comes suddenly or otherwise—is whether it serves to transform a person. I myself am more impressed by someone who can ask for help, or exhibit trust—someone who can work the 12 Steps of A.A.—than by someone who claims to have sighted an angel.

A spiritual awakening might be something stunning or it might be something much more pedestrian, but the real measure of a spiritual awakening may well be the lasting influence it has on a person.

What the Church Might Learn from A.A.

I am both a member of the church and a devotee of the philosophy of the 12 Steps. I like to think that the Alcoholics Anonymous program (along with the other 12-Step fellowships) complements Christian discipleship rather neatly.

The A.A. movement, historically, is indebted to the church. The 12-Step approach to recovery from addictions grew out of the Oxford Group. On one hand, A.A. borrowed many of its principles from the expression of the church called the Oxford Group; on the other hand, I believe that the church of today, in turn, could learn a few things from A.A.

In A.A., there is a general prohibition against using the words *should*, *ought*, and *must*. These verbs are firmly entrenched in our vernacular, of course, but they are used advisedly, if at all, by those who subscribe to the philosophy of the 12 Steps. *Should*, *ought*, and *must* tend to be shaming words. When people use these words, they often seek to diminish other people, or else they serve to put down the speakers themselves. As these three words are roughly synonymous, let the focus be narrowed to the word *should* alone.

If you were to state, "I *should* have gone to college twenty years ago," in effect, you would be indicting yourself, primarily by the use of the word *should*. If you were to leave out the *should*, however, you could say, matter-of-factly, "I *did not* go to college twenty years ago." Without the *should*, the sentence sounds less blaming, and more accepting.

When a person remarks, "I *should* go on a diet," that person, however subtly, has pointed an accusatory finger at himself or herself. Without that nasty *should*, the same person could vow, "I *shall* go on a diet."

When you employ the word *should* in reference to someone else, you risk judging that person by your own standards. You probably are talking down to another person when you assert, "You *should* go to marriage counseling." A more respectful

149

approach would omit the *should* altogether: "Maybe it would be helpful for you to go to marriage counseling."

Church folks may or may not be aware of the impact of a word like *should*—but the A.A. program has a way of sensitizing people to such a term. Whether or not the word *should* itself is pronounced in Christian circles, sometimes I detect in the church an "implied" *should*. Regardless of whether the word *should* is spoken out loud, a classic example is the notion that Christians *should* go to worship services every Sunday.

I have known a great many alcoholics who want nothing to do with the church because they react to the *should* of the church. It is ironic, but some people do not go to worship services precisely because of the prevailing idea that they are supposed to do so. The harder the church strives to get people to do what they *should*, the more vigorously some people resist.

This brings to mind another thing that the church might learn from A.A. Tradition 11 of the A.A. program states that A.A. relies upon the public relations policy of "attraction rather than promotion." In other words, A.A. does not attempt to sell itself to the public, to drum up membership, or to twist people's arms to get them to come to meetings. Rather than *promoting* itself, A.A. offers itself to the community as a worthwhile organization, something *attractive*.

What exactly is the difference between *attraction* and *promotion*? I shall let you ponder this for yourselves. I myself believe, however, that the church needs to do less *shoulding,* less *shaming*, less *promoting*—and more in the way of upholding people as being intrinsically worthy of respect, and revering the Gospel story as something downright interesting, indeed, something *attractive*.

This is what the church might learn from A.A.

Workaholism

"More enslaving than our occupations, however,
are our preoccupations."
(Henri Nouwen[95])

Bernie was a hard worker. He put in some long days as a mechanic at a factory. Bernie (not his real name) sometimes toiled 60 to 70 hours per week, including the double shifts he often was asked to perform. He must have been an indispensable fixture on the job; frequently, he was called in to work in the dead of night when something broke down that no one else could repair.

Bernie had not had a vacation in 32 years. His company allowed him to take some extra pay in lieu of his vacation time.

Aside from his job at the factory, Bernie also mowed lawns for quite a few of his neighbors. In all, he tried to keep up with about 25 lawns, which sometimes meant that he was hard at work until almost midnight. He was proud to say that he had been able to pay off his new rider-mower in just two summers.

Bernie was a hard worker. He was a *driven* man. He could not sit still. He had to keep busy. Bernie was a classic workaholic.

He was also an alcoholic. The two problems often fit together rather snugly.

Bernie never had time for hobbies or recreation. He was too restless for such things. According to his wife, Bernie's motto was: "If it doesn't make money, it doesn't count."

Bernie often complained about how busy he was, but he still found time to drink, either at the liquor store after his shift at the factory, or in the basement of his home. Although he claimed that he did not have any leisure, the truth was that he did have some spare time, and he devoted it to drinking.

There is some kind of affinity between workaholism and alcoholism. The parallel between them is obvious: the preoccupation with work and the preoccupation with booze. I

151

would not care to argue that workaholism leads to alcoholism, but a slavish devotion to duty certainly can set the stage for alcoholism. There is some evidence that our society is getting serious about addressing alcoholism, but many people still dismiss the problem of workaholism with a chuckle.

There is an old saying that goes like this: "Work doesn't love you back." Family members or friends might reciprocate your love, but work does not love you back. A pet could return your affection. Even a hobby may reward you. In the long run, however, work does not love people back.

If you have a job, you have something valuable. Work and income are important, but they are not all-important. When work—or, for that matter, alcohol—becomes the most meaningful thing in life, something is out of focus. Ultimately, work will not love you back. Alcohol has a way of turning on people, too.

This much Bernie learned for himself. He found that sobriety, for him, meant allowing for some leisure time in his schedule. He discovered that he needed to keep work in its proper perspective: It is important, but not as important as his life and health and family.

"There are 24 hours in each day," mused a recovering alcoholic. "There are eight hours in which to work, eight hours to sleep, and eight hours to pray and play and go to A.A." Maybe this scheme would not work for everyone. Perhaps it sounds too simplistic, or even *corny*. Still, it does put work and rest and self-care into an intriguing perspective.

And it rhymes.

You Do Not Have to Answer the Telephone Every Time it Rings

Once there was a man who had a "thing" about telephones. He was 75, and a steady drinker. This man insisted that a telephone should never be permitted to ring twice.

This fellow had accumulated a half-dozen telephones, and positioned them in strategic locations around his small house, so that they would be easily accessible. In this man's mind, it was desperately important that a telephone be answered before it rang for the second time.

Now, the odd thing about this man was that he himself refused to pick up the telephone, although he never did say why. He demanded that his dutiful wife and his adult daughter (who lived with her parents) respond to the telephone—and with all due haste, too. If the phone was not answered promptly, he became belligerent. When the phone rang for the second time, which was not allowed to happen very often, he would lean forward in his easy chair, and bring his cane down on the coffee table with a terrible "thwack!"

His wife and daughter knew precisely what this meant. They understood the urgency of the situation. The older man wanted someone to pick up the phone right away. If you do not answer the phone promptly, people might think you are rude—or so the man claimed.

I think I can understand this man's insistence that the phone be answered with dispatch. Sort of. I think I can understand why his wife and daughter would jump whenever they heard the sound of the telephone, too. Call it a conditioned response.

The jangle of a telephone calls to something deep within a person. It appeals to instinct. It comes as a demand. It taps into some primal sense of obligation. When the phone rings, it seizes our attention, and becomes the single most important thing in our world.

153

It is highly unnatural to refrain from picking up the receiver of a telephone that is ringing before you. It stirs up all sorts of feelings—like guilt (What if someone knew you were ignoring this call?) or anxiety (What if it is an emergency?) and even hope (What if this call is really good news?).

Some people feel compelled to pounce at a ringing telephone, but I have come to admire people who show restraint about such things. After all, you do have a choice. Many people feel a deep need to answer the phone, but there is an even deeper truth that is discussed sometimes in Al-Anon circles: You don't have to answer the telephone every time it rings.

Think of it. There is no federal or state law that requires a citizen to reach for a telephone whenever it stirs. More importantly, there is no reason that you have to *react* to other people, even those who try strenuously to evoke your fear or guilt or anger. You do not have to react as others expect, even though they brandish an angry cane.

You do not have to answer the telephone every time it rings. When others seek to "push your buttons," you do not have to respond. You have a choice. If someone attempts to bait you into an argument, it is up to you whether you wish to participate.

I expect that the elderly man in the easy chair is going to continue to slam his stick on the coffee table as long as it gets the results he desires. If his wife and daughter would point out to the man that he is capable of answering the telephone himself, something in that family system would change, and probably for the better.

Do you suppose this jingle will ever become an official Al-Anon slogan? "You don't have to answer the telephone every time it rings."

Endnotes

[1]*Came to Believe…The Spiritual Adventure of A.A. as Experienced by Individual Members* (New York: Alcoholics Anonymous World Services, Inc., 1973), p. 59

[2]Thomas Merton, *Conjectures of a Guilty Bystander* (Garden City, New York: Doubleday & Company, Inc., 1966), p. 73.

[3]Odd S. Lovoll, *The Promise of America: A History of the Norwegian-American People* (Minneapolis: University of Minnesota Press, 1984), p. 102.

[4]Lovoll, p. 104.

[5]*Alcoholics Anonymous*, 3rd ed. (New York: Alcoholics Anonymous World Services, Inc., 1976), p. 98.

[6]*As Bill Sees It: The A.A. Way of Life* (New York: Alcoholics Anonymous World Services, Inc., 1967), p. 84.

[7]*As Bill Sees It*, p. 177.

[8]*Lois Remembers: Memoirs of the Co-founder of Al-Anon and Wife of the Co-founder of Alcoholics Anonymous* (New York: Al-Anon Family Group Headquarters, Inc., 1979), p. 126.

[9]*Dr. Bob and the Good Oldtimers: A Biography, with Recollections of Early A.A., in the Midwest* (New York: Alcoholics Anonymous World Services, Inc., 1980), p. 97.

[10]*Twenty-Four Hours a Day* (Center City, Minnesota: Hazelden Foundation, 1975), May 15.

Gregory P. Gabriel

[11]Ernest Kurtz, *Not-God: A History of Alcoholics Anonymous* (Center City, Minnesota: Hazelden Educational Materials, 1979), p. 48.

[12]Nan Robertson, *Getting Better: Inside Alcoholics Anonymous* (New York: William Morrow & Company, Inc., 1988), p. 59.

[13]*'Pass It On': The Story of Bill Wilson and How the A.A. Message Reached the World* (New York: Alcoholics Anonymous World Services, Inc., 1984), p. 170.

[14]*Dr. Bob and the Good Oldtimers*, p. 155.

[15]*'Pass It On,'* p. 387.

[16]*John Bakeless, ed., The Journals of Lewis and Clark (New York: Mentor, 1964), p. 90*

[17]*As Bill Sees It*, p. 278.

[18]*Dr. Bob and the Good Oldtimers*, p. 264.

[19]*'Pass It On,'* p. 172.

[20]Robertson, p. 36.

[21]Robertson, p. 84.

[22]Sam Keen, *Fire in the Belly: On Being a Man* (New York: Bantam Books, 1992), p. 108.

[23]*Twenty-Four Hours a Day*, July 23.

[24]*'Pass It On,'* p. 371.

[25]Henri J. M. Nouwen, *Making All Things New: An Invitation to the Spiritual Life* (San Francisco: Harper & Row, Publishers, Inc., 1981), p. 30.

[26]*Twenty-Four Hours a Day*, February 3.

[27]*Twelve Steps and Twelve Traditions,* p. 27.

[28]*As Bill Sees It*, p. 191.

[29]*As Bill Sees It*, p. 73.

[30]*Dr. Bob and the Good Oldtimers*, p. 166.

[31]N.T. Wright, *The Lord & His Prayer* (Grand Rapids, Michigan: William B. Eerdmans Publishing Company, 1996), p. 88.

[32]*Came to Believe...*, page 73.

[33]*One Day at a Time in Al-Anon* (New York: Al-Anon Family Group Headquarters, Inc., 1973), p. 48.

[34]*'Pass It On,'* p. 241.

[35]*'Pass It On,'* pp. 242-3.

[36]*'Pass It On,'* p. 243.

[37]*'Pass It On,'* p. 243.

[38]*Twelve Steps and Twelve Traditions*, p. 60.

[39]*Came to Believe...*, p. 30.

[40]*Came to Believe...*, p. 48.

[41]*Dr. Bob and the Good Oldtimers*, p. 194.

[42]*Alcoholics Anonymous*, p. 570.

[43]*Alcoholics Anonymous*, p. 550.

[44]*Came to Believe...*, p. 97.

[45]*Alcoholics Anonymous*, pp. 569-70.

[46]*Alcoholics Anonymous*, p. 570.

[47]*Alcoholics Anonymous*, p. 49.

[48]*Came to Believe...*, p. 64.

[49]*Dr. Bob and the Good Oldtimers*, p. 85.

[50]Kurtz, p. 70.

[51]Harry M. Tiebout, M.D., "The Ego Factors in Surrender in Alcoholism," *Quarterly Journal of Studies on Alcohol*, 15, (1954), 621.

[52]H. George Anderson, *A Good Time to be the Church: A Conversation with Bishop H. George Anderson* (Minneapolis: Augsburg Fortress, 1997), p. 20.

[53]Kathleen Norris, *Amazing Grace: A Vocabulary of Faith* (New York: Riverhead Books, 1998), p. 258.

[54]*Courage to Change: One Day at a Time in Al-Anon II* (New York: Al-Anon Family Group Headquarters, Inc., 1992), p. 223.

[55]Gerhard von Rad, *Genesis: A Commentary,* rev. ed. (Philadelphia: The Westminster Press, 1972), p. 241.

[56]Patricia Hampl, *Virgin Time* (New York: Ballantine Books, 1992), p. 35.

[57]Robertson, p. 60.

[58]*'Pass It On,'* p. 124.

[59]*Alcoholics Anonymous*, p. 569.

[60]Bill Wilson, *Three Talks to Medical Societies by Bill W., Co-founder of A.A.* (New York: Alcoholics Anonymous World Services, Inc.), p. 15.

[61]*Came to Believe...*, p. 84.

[62]*As We Understood...: A Collection of Spiritual Insights by Al-Anon and Alateen Members* (New York: Al-Anon Family Group Headquarters, Inc., 1990), p. 159.

[63]*Twenty-Four Hours a Day*, March 25.

[64]Kurtz, p. 99.

[65]*Just for Today* (New York: Al-Anon Family Group Headquarters, Inc., 1972).

[66]William James, *The Varieties of Religious Experience: A Study in Human Nature* (New York: New American Library), p. 297.

[67]*One Day at a Time in Al-Anon*, p. 258.

[68]*A New Beginning* (Los Angeles: The G.A. Publishing Company, 1989), p. 38.

[69]*'Pass It On,'* p. 136.

[70]*Lois Remembers*, p. 27.

[71]*One Day at a Time in Al-Anon*, p. 356.

[72]*Came to Believe...*, p. 81.

[73]C.S. Lewis, *The Problem of Pain: How Human Suffering Raises Almost Intolerable Intellectual Problems* (New York: Macmillan Publishing Co., Inc., 1962), p. 10.

[74]Stephen E. Ambrose, *Undaunted Courage: Meriwether Lewis, Thomas Jefferson, and the Opening of the American West* (New York: Simon & Schuster Inc., 1996), p. 312.

[75]*Alcoholics Anonymous Comes of Age: A Brief History of A.A.* (New York: Alcoholics Anonymous World Services, Inc., 1957), p. 258.

[76]*Alcoholics Anonymous Comes of Age*, p. 264.

[77]*Alcoholics Anonymous Comes of Age*, p. 183.

[78]*Alcoholics Anonymous Comes of Age*, p. 324.

[79]*Alcoholics Anonymous*, p. 570.

[80]Dietrich Bonhoeffer, *Life Together* (San Francisco: Harper & Row, Publishers, Inc., 1954), p. 41.

[81]*'Pass It On,'* p. 184.

[82]Kurtz, p. 205.

[83]Harry M. Tiebout, M.D., *The Act of Surrender in the Therapeutic Process* (New York: The National Council on Alcoholism), p. 3.

[84]*Twenty-Four Hours a Day*, July 16.

[85]*Alcoholics Anonymous*, p. 82.

[86]*Alcoholics Anonymous*, pp. 58-9.

[87]*Alcoholics Anonymous*, p. 164.

[88]*Alcoholics Anonymous*, p. 56.

[89]*Alcoholics Anonymous Comes of Age*, p. 312.

[90]'*Pass It On,'* p. 121.

[91]*Dr. Bob and the Good Oldtimers*, p. 307.

[92]*Alcoholics Anonymous*, p. 569.

[93]*Alcoholics Anonymous*, p. 569.

[94]*Alcoholics Anonymous*, p. 569.

[95]Nouwen, p. 25.

Gregory P. Gabriel

Appendix A

The 12 Steps of Alcoholics Anonymous

1. We admitted we were powerless over alcohol—that our lives had become unmanageable.

2. Came to believe that a Power greater than ourselves could restore us to sanity.

3. Made a decision to turn our will and our lives over to the care of God as we understood Him.

4. Made a searching and fearless moral inventory of ourselves.

5. Admitted to God, to ourselves, and to another human being, the exact nature of our wrongs.

6. Were entirely ready to have God remove all these defects of character.

7. Humbly asked Him to remove our shortcomings.

8. Made a list of all persons we had harmed, and became willing to make amends to them all.

9. Made direct amends to such people whenever possible, except when to do so would injure them or others.

10. Continued to take personal inventory and when we were wrong promptly admitted it.

Gregory P. Gabriel

11. Sought through prayer and meditation to improve our conscious contact with God as we understood Him, praying only for knowledge of His will for us and the power to carry that out.

12. Having had a spiritual awakening as the result of these steps, we tried to carry this message to alcoholics, and to practice these principles in all our affairs.

Appendix B

The 12 Traditions of Alcoholics Anonymous

1. Our common welfare should come first; personal recovery depends upon A.A. unity.

2. For our group purpose there is but one ultimate authority—a loving God as He may express Himself in our group conscience. Our leaders are but trusted servants—they do not govern.

3. The only requirement for A.A. membership is a desire to stop drinking.

4. Each group should be autonomous, except in matters affecting other groups or A.A. as a whole.

5. Each group has but one primary purpose—to carry its message to the alcoholic who still suffers.

6. An A.A. group ought never endorse, finance, or lend the A.A. name to any related facility or outside enterprise lest problems of money, property and prestige divert us from our primary purpose.

7. Every A.A. group ought to be fully self-supporting, declining outside contributions.

8. Alcoholics Anonymous should remain forever non-professional, but our service centers may employ special workers.

9. A.A., as such, ought never to be organized, but we may create service boards or committees directly responsible to those they serve.

10. Alcoholics Anonymous has no opinion on outside issues, hence the A.A. name ought never be drawn into public controversy.

11. Our public relations policy is based on attraction rather than promotion; we need always maintain personal anonymity at the level of press, radio, and films.

12. Anonymity is the spiritual foundation of all our traditions, ever reminding us to place principles before personalities.

Appendix C

The 12 Steps of Gamblers Anonymous

1. We admitted we were powerless over gambling—that our lives had become unmanageable.

2. Came to believe that a Power greater than ourselves could restore us to a normal way of thinking and living.

3. Made a decision to turn our will and our lives over to the care of this Power of our own understanding.

4. Made a searching and fearless moral and financial inventory of ourselves.

5. Admitted to ourselves and to another human being the exact nature of our wrongs.

6. Were entirely ready to have these defects of character removed.

7. Humbly asked God (of our understanding) to remove our shortcomings.

8. Made a list of all persons we had harmed and became willing to make amends to them all.

9. Made direct amends to such people wherever possible, except when to do so would injure them or others.

10. Continued to take personal inventory and when we were wrong, promptly admitted it.

11. Sought through prayer and meditation to improve our conscious contact with God as we understood Him, praying only for knowledge of His will for us and the power to carry that out.

12. Having made an effort to practice these principles in all our affairs, we tried to carry this message to other compulsive gamblers.

Bibliography

A New Beginning. Los Angeles: The G.A. Publishing Company, 1989.

Al-Anon Family Groups. New York: Al-Anon Family Group Headquarters, Inc., 1955.

Alcoholics Anonymous. 3rd ed. New York: Alcoholics Anonymous World Services, Inc., 1976.

Alcoholics Anonymous Comes of Age: A Brief History of A.A. New York: Alcoholics Anonymous World Services, Inc., 1957.

Alcoholism: The Family Disease. New York: Al-Anon Family Group Headquarters, Inc., 1972.

Ambrose, Stephen E. *Undaunted Courage: Meriwether Lewis, Thomas Jefferson, and the Opening of the American West.* New York: Simon & Schuster Inc., 1996.

Anderson, H. George. *A Good Time to be the Church: A Conversation with Bishop H. George Anderson.* Minneapolis: Augsburg Fortress, 1997.

As Bill Sees It: The A.A. Way of Life. New York: Alcoholics Anonymous World Services, Inc., 1967.

As We Understood...: A Collection of Spiritual Insights by Al-Anon and Alateen Members. New York: Al-Anon Family Group Headquarters, Inc., 1990.

B., Mel. *New Wine: The Spiritual Roots of the Twelve Step Miracle.* Center City, Minnesota: Hazelden Foundation, 1991.

Bakeless, John, ed. *The Journals of Lewis and Clark*. New York: Mentor, 1964.

Bonhoeffer, Dietrich. *Life Together*. San Francisco: Harper & Row, Publishers, Inc., 1954.

Came to Believe...: The Spiritual Adventure of A.A. as Experienced by Individual Members. New York: Alcoholics Anonymous World Services, Inc., 1973.

Clark, Walter Houston. *The Oxford Group: Its History and Significance*. New York: Bookman Associates, Inc., 1951.

Courage to Change: One Day at a Time in Al-Anon II. New York: Al-Anon Family Group Headquarters, Inc., 1992.

Dr. Bob and the Good Oldtimers: A Biography, with Recollections of Early A.A. in the Midwest. New York: Alcoholics Anonymous World Services, Inc., 1980.

Guelzo, Allen C. *Abraham Lincoln: Redeemer President*. Grand Rapids, Michigan: William B. Eerdmans Publishing Company, 1999.

Hampl, Patricia. *Virgin Time*. New York: Ballantine Books, 1992.

James, William. *The Varieties of Religious Experience: A Study in Human Nature*. New York: New American Library.

Just For Today. New York: Al-Anon Family Group Headquarters, Inc., 1972.

Keen, Sam. *Fire in the Belly: On Being a Man*. New York: Bantam Books, 1992.

Kurtz, Ernest. *Not-God: A History of Alcoholics Anonymous*. Center City, Minnesota: Hazelden Educational Materials, 1979.

Lewis, C.S. *The Problem of Pain: How Human Suffering Raises Almost Intolerable Intellectual Problems*. New York: Macmillan Publishing Co., Inc., 1962.

Lois Remembers: Memoirs of the Co-founder of Al-Anon and Wife of the Co-founder of Alcoholics Anonymous. New York: Al-Anon Family Group Headquarters, Inc., 1979.

Lovoll, Odd S. *The Promise of America: A History of the Norwegian-American People*. Minneapolis: University of Minnesota Press, 1984.

Merton, Thomas. *Conjectures of a Guilty Bystander*. Garden City, New York: Doubleday & Company, Inc., 1966.

Norris, Kathleen. *Amazing Grace: A Vocabulary of Faith*. New York: The Berkley Publishing Group, 1998.

Nouwen, Henri J. M. *Making All Things New: An Invitation to the Spiritual Life*. San Francisco: Harper & Row, Publishers, Inc., 1981.

One Day at a Time in Al-Anon. New York: Al-Anon Family Group Headquarters, Inc., 1973.

'Pass It On': The Story of Bill Wilson and How the A.A. Message Reached the World. New York: Alcoholics Anonymous World Services, Inc., 1984.

Rad, Gerhard von. *Genesis: A Commentary*. Rev. ed. Philadelphia: The Westminster Press, 1972.

171

Gregory P. Gabriel

Robertson, Nan. *Getting Better: Inside Alcoholics Anonymous*. New York: William Morrow and Company, Inc., 1988.

Russel, A. J. *For Sinners Only*. New York: Harper & Brothers Publishers, 1932.

Shedler, Jonathan and Jack Block. "Adolescent Drug Use and Psychological Health: A Longitudinal Inquiry." *American Psychologist*, 45 (May 1990), 612-30.

The Layman with a Notebook, *What Is the Oxford Group?* New York: Oxford University Press, 1933.

Tiebout, Harry M., M.D. "The Ego Factors in Surrender in Alcoholism." *Quarterly Journal of Studies on Alcohol*, 15 (1954), 610-21.

Tiebout, Harry M., M.D. *The Act of Surrender in the Therapeutic Process*. New York: The National Council on Alcoholism.

Twelve Steps and Twelve Traditions. New York: Alcoholics Anonymous World Services, Inc., 1952.

Twenty-Four Hours a Day. Center City, Minnesota: Hazelden Foundation, 1975.

Westberg, Granger E. *Good Grief: A Constructive Approach to the Problem of Loss*. Philadelphia: Fortress Press, 1962.

Wilson, Bill. *Three Talks to Medical Societies by Bill W., Co-founder of A.A.* New York: Alcoholics Anonymous World Services, Inc.

Wright, N.T. *The Lord & His Prayer*. Grand Rapids, Michigan: William B. Eerdmans Publishing Company, 1996.

About the Author

A pastor of the Evangelical Lutheran Church in America, The Reverend Greg Gabriel has been working in the field of addictions for the past 14 years. He serves part-time as a chaplain at Project Turnabout, which is a treatment center for chemically dependent people and compulsive gamblers in Granite Falls, Minnesota, and part-time as the pastor of Jevnaker and Mandt Lutheran Churches of rural Montevideo, Minnesota. Pastor Gabriel participated in four quarters of Clinical Pastoral Education at Hazelden (a chemical dependency treatment center near Center City, Minnesota) and also was employed as a family counselor at Hazelden. He has done a variety of presentations and writings on the topic of spirituality and recovery from addictions.

Pastor Gabriel is a native of Hector, Minnesota. He is a graduate of Concordia College in Moorhead, Minnesota, and of Luther Seminary in St. Paul, Minnesota. He also has served as the pastor of a rural parish in Nebraska. His wife is Joanne; their sons are Tim and Chris.